FOUR SEASONS
of BEADiNG™

Edited by Barb Switzer

Annie's
Attic®

Four Seasons of Beading™

Copyright © 2009 DRG

EDITOR	Barb Switzer
ART DIRECTOR	Brad Snow
PUBLISHING SERVICES DIRECTOR	Brenda Gallmeyer
ASSISTANT ART DIRECTOR	Nick Pierce
MANAGING EDITOR	Barb Sprunger
COPY SUPERVISOR	Michelle Beck
COPY EDITOR	Amanda Ladig
TECHNICAL EDITOR	Brooke Smith
PHOTOGRAPHY SUPERVISOR	Tammy Christian
PHOTOGRAPHY	Matthew Owen
PHOTO STYLIST	Tammy Steiner
GRAPHIC ARTS SUPERVISOR	Ronda Bechinski
GRAPHIC ARTISTS	Glenda Chamberlain, Edith Teegarden
PRODUCTION ASSISTANTS	Marj Morgan, Judy Neuenschwander

Printed in the United States of America
First Printing: 2009
Library of Congress Control Number: 2009903106
ISBN: 978-1-59635-267-4

AnniesAttic.com

1 2 3 4 5 6 7 8 9

WELCOME

"Live each season as it passes; breathe the air, drink the drink, taste the fruit, and resign yourself to the influences of each." —Henry David Thoreau

Instead of using a crystal ball to predict the fashion for this year, work with classic color trends and holiday themes to make stunning jewelry in a snap. Color swatches set the mood for summer, spring, winter and fall, marking the changing weather, trends and palettes.

Beginners can see all the materials, tools and techniques in the photo glossary and step-by-step instructions. Intermediate beaders can easily complete any project in the book. Beautiful photos showcase the unique style of every project and show the details to make creating your own jewelry simple.

Celebrate the holidays with glass, ceramic, semi-precious stones, pearls, crystals, shells and even wood. Make bracelets, necklaces and earrings, and be inspired to try new colors and expand your jewelry collection to fit what you wear every day of the year.

BARB

CONTENTS

SPRiNG

SUMMER

FALL

WiNTER

ALL SEASONS

ViSUAL GLOSSARY

TOOLS

Crimping pliers are for just what their name implies, crimping! The back slot puts a seam in the middle of the crimp tube, separating the ends of the flex wire and trapping it firmly. The front slot rounds out the tube and turns it into a small, tidy bead.

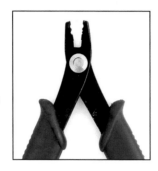

Chain-nose pliers are the most useful tool in your entire toolbox. For holding, opening and closing jump rings and bending sharp angles.

Round-nose pliers are intended for turning round loops. They do not work well for holding or grasping since they tend to leave a small dent.

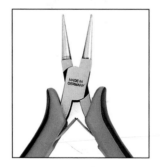

Flat-nose pliers are a wire power tool. They are excellent for turning sharp corners, holding items and for opening and closing jump rings.

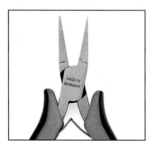

Wire flush cutters leave one flat side and one pointed side on each cut. Using flush cutters is especially important when working with heavy gauges of wire (20-gauge or smaller). One side of the cutter is flat and the other is indented.

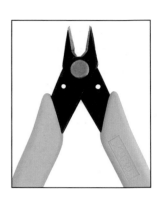

Nylon-jaw pliers can be used to harden or straighten wire.

Jeweler's hammers have fine, smooth curved heads to leave a clean impression. The round peen side works well for texturing wire and metal sheet.

A bench block is a flat, smooth piece of hardened steel. Hammering on top of a block flattens out and hardens the wire. Bench blocks are also used for stamping metal to get a clean impression.

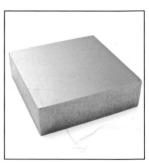

MATERIALS

Eye Pins are wires with a loop on one end and a straight portion of wire where beads can be strung. Length and gauges vary; most earrings use 24-gauge eye pins from 1½–2½ inches.

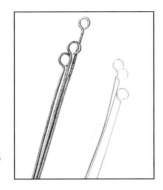

Head Pins are a piece of wire with a stop end like a fine nail head. A bead slides onto the head pin and stops on the head. Lengths and gauges vary; most earrings use 24-gauge head pins from 1½–2½ inches.

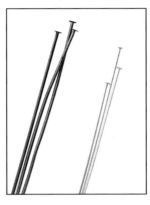

Jump Rings are one of the most versatile findings used in jewelry-making. They come in all sizes, gauges and metals. They are measured by diameter (width) and gauge (weight).

Ear Wires come in many different styles. Regular fishhook style are the most common and the easiest to make yourself. Recommended weight for ear wires is either 22- or 20-gauge.

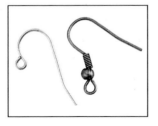

Crimp Tubes are small soft metal cylinders that can be flattened or formed around flexible beading wire to secure the ends. They are an essential component for bead stringing projects.

Wire comes in many sizes or *gauges*. Gauge is the measured diameter of the wire. The higher the number, the thinner the wire. Wire can be tempered soft, half-hard or hard, which refers to its stiffness. Copper, silver and gold-filled are most commonly used for jewelry.

Flexible Beading Wire comes in several weights from .010–.026-inch-diameter and is designed for stringing. It is available in precious metal and several colors and is made from 7 to 49 strands of steel wire, twisted and encased in a flexible plastic coating. Ends are finished with crimp beads using either crimping or chain-nose pliers.

BASiCS STEP BY STEP

Creating your own beaded jewelry is easy and only takes a few tools. Practice these techniques using less expensive metal findings. Once your finishing techniques are perfected, use real sterling silver or vermeil (real gold plating over sterling silver) to add elegance to your beadwork.

OPENING & CLOSING JUMP RINGS

Jump rings are one of the most versatile findings used in jewelry-making. They come in all sizes and gauges.

Use two pairs of smooth chain-nose pliers (bent or flat-nose pliers work fine as a second plier). (Photo A)

Photo A

Push ring open with right plier while holding across the ring with left plier. To close, hold in the same way and rock the ring back and forth until ring ends rub against each other or you hear a click. Moving the ring past closed then back hardens the ring and assures a tight closure. (Photo B)

Photo B

MAKING AN EYE PIN OR ROUND LOOP

Eye pins should be made with half-hard wire to make sure they hold their shape. 22-gauge will fit through most beads, with the exception of many semi-precious stones. Most Czech glass beads and 4mm crystals will fit on 20-gauge wire.

The length used for the eye loop depends on how big you want the loop. Here we will use ⅜ inch for a moderate size loop.

Flush trim end of wire. (Photo A)

Photo A   **Photo B**

Using chain-nose pliers, make a 90-degree bend ⅜ inch from end of wire. (Photo B)

Using round-nose pliers, grasp the end of the wire so no wire sticks out between plier blades. (Photo C)

Photo C

Begin making a loop by rolling your hand away from your body. Don't try to make the entire loop in one movement. Roll your hand ¼ turn counterclockwise. (Photo D)

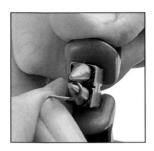

Photo D

Without removing pliers from loop, open plier blade slightly and pivot plier back toward your body clockwise about ¼ turn. (Photo E)

Photo E

Close plier onto the wire and roll the loop until it comes around, next to the 90-degree bend. (Photo F)

Open and close eye-pin loops the same way as jump rings, by pushing open front to back. (Photo G)

Photo F

Photo G

MAKING WIRE-WRAPPED LOOPS

Practice wire wrapping with either 22- or 24-gauge wire. Harden slightly by pulling on one end with the other end clamped in a vise, or pull one or two times through nylon-jaw pliers. (Photo A)

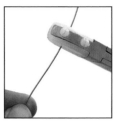

Photo A

Make a 90-degree bend about 1½ inches from end of the wire using chain-nose pliers. (Photo B)

Photo B

Using round-nose pliers, grab wire about ⅜ inch away from the 90-degree and roll your hand away from yourself, toward the bend until a loop is halfway formed. (Photos C and D)

Photo C   **Photo D**

Without removing plier from forming loop, open the jaw and rotate plier clockwise about ¼ turn. (Photo E)

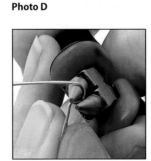

Photo E

Grab the end of the wire with your left (non-dominant) hand and pull it around the rest of the way until it crosses itself and completes the loop. (Photo F)

Photo F

Switch to chain-nose pliers, holding across the loop. Wrap tail around wire under loop with your left hand. If you are using a heavy wire gauge, it is often easier to use a second plier to pull the tail around instead of your fingers. (Photos G and H)

Photo G

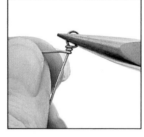

Photo H

Flush cut wire as close to the wrap as possible. Tuck end down if needed, using chain-nose pliers. (Photos I and J)

Photo I

Photo J

To create a wrap on the opposite end of the bead, leave a gap equal to wrap space on first end. Grasp to the right of the wrap space and make a 90-degree bend. (Photos K and L)

Photo K

Photo L

Repeat from Photo C–L to complete.

HAMMERING WIRE

Hammering hardens and flattens round wire. This can be especially important when making ear wires or clasps that need to hold their shape. Always use a smooth, hardened steel surface to guarantee a clean finish. Any marks or scars on a bench block or hammer will impress on the surface of wire or sheet metal.

Create your shape from wire. Keep hammer flat to prevent marring wire. Flip over after a few taps and hammer on opposite side. Don't get carried away, if you hammer too much metal becomes brittle and breaks. (Photo A)

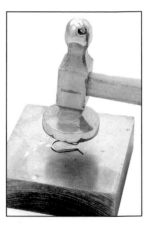

Photo A

CRIMPING

String a crimp bead onto flexible wire. String clasp or ring and pass tail of flexible wire back through crimp to form a loop.

Hold wires parallel and make sure crimp is positioned correctly. Using front slot on plier, shape crimp into a small oval. (Photo A)

Photo A

Put oval into back slot of plier and squeeze to make fold in the center with one wire on each side of fold. (Photo B)

Photo B

Return to front slot, and squeeze again to tighten crimp. Do a few more rotations and squeezes to solidify and shape crimp bead. Trim wire tail. (Photo C)

Photo C

METRiC CONVERSiON CHARTS

METRIC CONVERSIONS

yards	x	.9144	=	metres (m)
yards	x	91.44	=	centimetres (cm)
inches	x	2.54	=	centimetres (cm)
inches	x	25.40	=	millimetres (mm)
inches	x	.0254	=	metres (m)

centimetres	x	.3937	=	inches
metres	x	1.0936	=	yards

INCHES INTO MILLIMETRES & CENTIMETRES (Rounded off slightly)

inches	mm	cm	inches	cm	inches	cm	inches	cm
1/8	3	0.3	5	12.5	21	53.5	38	96.5
1/4	6	0.6	5 1/2	14	22	56	39	99
3/8	10	1	6	15	23	58.5	40	101.5
1/2	13	1.3	7	18	24	61	41	104
5/8	15	1.5	8	20.5	25	63.5	42	106.5
3/4	20	2	9	23	26	66	43	109
7/8	22	2.2	10	25.5	27	68.5	44	112
1	25	2.5	11	28	28	71	45	114.5
1 1/4	32	3.2	12	30.5	29	73.5	46	117
1 1/2	38	3.8	13	33	30	76	47	119.5
1 3/4	45	4.5	14	35.5	31	79	48	122
2	50	5	15	38	32	81.5	49	124.5
2 1/2	65	6.5	16	40.5	33	84	50	127
3	75	7.5	17	43	34	86.5		
3 1/2	90	9	18	46	35	89		
4	100	10	19	48.5	36	91.5		
4 1/2	115	11.5	20	51	37	94		

SPRiNG

Soft pastel and swaths of flowery bright color draw your mood to this season of renewal. Celebrate Easter, St. Patrick's Day, Earth Day, Mother's Day and May Day.

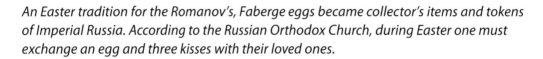

beginner

A HUG &
THREE KiSSES

Design by Rupa Balachandar

An Easter tradition for the Romanov's, Faberge eggs became collector's items and tokens of Imperial Russia. According to the Russian Orthodox Church, during Easter one must exchange an egg and three kisses with their loved ones.

INSTRUCTIONS

1) String a crimp bead onto wire 1½ inches from one end. Thread short wire tail through a clear crystal, Wire Guardian and one half of clasp; insert short wire back through crystal and crimp bead. Use crimp pliers to flatten crimp bead.

2) String a daisy spacer and seven pink opal beads.

3) String a seed bead and a pink opal bead. Repeat seven more times.

4) String a seed bead, light peach crystal, seed bead, pink opal bead, seed bead, light peach crystal and a seed bead.

5) String a pink opal bead, seed bead, daisy spacer, Caribbean blue opal crystal, daisy spacer, seed bead, pink opal bead, seed bead, daisy spacer, padparadscha crystal, daisy spacer and a seed bead. Repeat once.

6) String a pink opal bead, seed bead, daisy spacer, Caribbean blue opal crystal and a seed bead.

7) String pendant.

8) Repeat steps 2–6 in reverse to complete other half of necklace.

9) String a crimp bead and a clear crystal; insert wire through a Wire Guardian and remaining half of clasp. Thread wire back through clear crystal and crimp bead. Flatten crimp bead. Trim excess wire. ●

Source: Pendant, beads, crystals and clasp from RupaB Designs.

MATERIALS

Faberge egg pendant with attached crystal
42 (7–8mm) pink opal round beads
44 (11/0) gold seed beads
20 (4mm) gold vermeil daisy spacers
4mm CRYSTALLIZED™ - Swarovski Elements bicone crystals:
  6 Caribbean blue opal,
  4 padparadscha,
  4 light peach, 2 clear

2 gold Wire Guardians
2 (2mm) gold-plated crimp beads
Gold-plated fluted pearl clasp
22 inches .019-inch-diameter nylon-coated flexible beading wire
Chain-nose pliers
Crimp pliers
Wire cutters

FINISHED SIZE

18½ inches (including clasp)

beginner

APRiL SHOWERS

Designs by Laura Stafford

Lustrous green pearls and shimmering shells capture the fresh essence of a spring shower.

INSTRUCTIONS

Necklace

1) Cut a 20-inch length of beading wire. String a crimp tube and a crystal onto wire 1 inch from one end. Thread short wire tail through Wire Guardian and loop on one half of clasp; insert wire back through crystal and crimp tube. Use crimp pliers to flatten and fold crimp tube.

2) String a crystal.

3) Beginning and ending with pearls, string 20 pearls and 19 seed beads alternating between the two.

4) String the following: crystal, sterling silver spacer, crystal and two pearls. Repeat once.

5) String three sterling silver round beads. String pendant on top of round beads.

6) Repeat steps 2–4 in reverse to complete other half of necklace.

7) String a crimp tube and a crystal. Thread wire through a Wire Guardian, loop on other half of clasp and back through crystal, crimp tube and crystal. Flatten and fold crimp tube. Trim excess wire.

Bracelet

1) Repeat step 1 of Necklace with remaining 9-inch length of wire.

2) String a crystal and three pearls.

3) String a crystal, sterling silver spacer, crystal and two pearls. Repeat three more times.

4) String a crystal, sterling silver spacer, crystal, three pearls and a crystal.

5) Repeat step 7 of Necklace. ●

Sources: Pearls from Majestic Pearl Inc.; CRYSTALLIZED™ - Swarovski Elements crystals from Brightlings Beads; sterling silver beads and seed beads from Fire Mountain Gems and Beads; sterling silver toggle clasp from Pegasus Imports; Paua shell toggle clasp from Tucson Mountain Jewelry/LS Designs; pendant from Sajen Inc.

MATERIALS

Aventurine/shell pendant
62 (6mm) green pearls
26 (4mm) green CRYSTALLIZED™ - Swarovski Elements bicone crystals
9 sterling silver Bali-style spacer beads
3 (2mm) sterling silver round beads
4 (2 x 2mm) sterling silver crimp tubes
4 sterling silver small Wire Guardians
Sterling silver toggle clasp
Sterling silver/Paua shell toggle clasp
29 inches .015-inch-diameter 49-strand nylon-coated flexible beading wire
Crimp pliers
Wire cutters

FINISHED SIZES

Necklace
17¾ inches (including clasp)
Bracelet
7¾ inches (including clasp)

intermediate

LUCK OF THE iRiSH

Design by Erin Strother

This brass pendant is sure to bring you compliments, if not good luck. Made with two beaded strands of wire twisted together, this necklace looks complicated, but works up quickly and is easily customized with beads from your existing stash.

INSTRUCTIONS

1) Cut an 8-inch length of bronze wire. String jade teardrop onto wire 1 inch from end. Bend wire ends centered above bead. Wrap short wire tail around base of long wire three times. Trim short wire tail. Form a wrapped loop with long wire tail, wrapping wire around previously-wrapped coils. Trim excess wire. Use chain-nose pliers to flatten wire end against bead. Open a jump ring and slide it onto wrapped loop; attach jump ring to bottom of clover pendant. Close ring.

2) Cut an 8-inch length of gold wire. Leaving a 1-inch tail, hold wire tail against back of clover stem near bottom; wrap wire around clover stem three times to anchor wire.

3) String a 3mm olivine round bead. Hold bead in place on top of stem and wrap wire tightly around stem. String another 3mm round bead and repeat. Continue stringing and wrapping until seven beads have been

strung. Wrap wire around stem three more times ending on back. Trim excess wire from both ends. Use chain-nose pliers to flatten ends against pendant.

4) Remove one link from chain and attach to top of pendant. Set aside.

5) Cut a 12-inch length of bronze wire. Form a wrapped loop at one end.

6) String three 3mm olivine round beads, bronze round bead and a dark green pearl. String 3½ inches of prehnite chips randomly inserting the following: one 6mm olivine round bead, dark green pearl,

Continued on page 35

MATERIALS

10 x 15mm olive jade
 teardrop bead
7 inches prehnite chips
Freshwater pearls: 3 (9mm) white,
 12 (3mm) white, 10 (7mm)
 pistachio, 12 (6mm) dark green
Fire-polished Czech glass
 round beads: 8 (6mm) olivine,
 42 (3mm) olivine,
 15 (4mm) bronze
2 (8mm) olive faceted
 round crystals
Brass clover pendant

7 (5mm) brass jump rings
Brass leaf toggle clasp
6¼ inches antique brass double
 cable chain
Craft wire: 20 inches 22-gauge
 bronze, 28 inches
 26-gauge gold
Round-nose pliers
Chain-nose pliers
Flush cutters

FINISHED SIZE

17 inches (including clasp)

intermediate

LADYBUG SPARKLE

Design by Melanie Brooks Lukacs, courtesy of Earthenwood Studio

A parade of ladybugs and bright crystal clusters will grace your wrist in this bracelet, designed to delight and bring sparkle to warm summer days.

INSTRUCTIONS

1) Slide a crystal and an 8/0 seed bead onto a head pin. Form a loop above beads. Trim excess wire. Repeat with each head pin.

2) Open loop on one beaded dangle and attach to a jump ring; close loop. Attach four more beaded dangles to same jump ring.

3) Repeat step 2 seven more times to attach five beaded dangles to each jump ring.

4) String a crimp tube onto beading wire ½ inch from one end. Insert short wire tail through loop on one half of clasp and back through crimp tube. Use crimp pliers to flatten and fold crimp tube. Cover crimp tube with a crimp cover.

5) String a heishi spacer and a ladybug.

6) String a heishi spacer, 6/0 seed bead, jump ring with beaded dangles, 6/0 seed bead, pewter floral bead, 6/0 seed bead, jump ring with beaded dangles, 6/0 seed bead, heishi spacer and a ladybug.

7) Repeat step 6 three more times. String a heishi spacer.

8) String a crimp tube. Thread wire through loop on other half of clasp and back through crimp tube. Flatten and fold crimp tube. Trim excess wire. Cover crimp tube with crimp cover.

9) Open loops and attach remaining four beaded dangles to loop on round half of clasp, two on each side of wire. Close loops. ●

Sources: Porcelain beads from Earthenwood Studio; crystals, seed beads, pewter beads, findings, clasp and beading wire from Fusion Beads.

MATERIALS
5 (15mm) orange/pink/melon porcelain ladybug beads
4 (8mm) pewter floral beads
44 (4mm) padparadscha CRYSTALLIZED™ - Swarovski Elements bicone crystals
Seed beads: 44 (8/0) orange colored-lined, 16 (6/0) orange
10 (4mm) pewter heishi spacer beads
8 (6mm) sterling silver closed jump rings
44 (1-inch) sterling silver head pins
2 (2 x 2mm) sterling silver crimp tubes
2 (3mm) sterling silver crimp covers
15 x 20mm pewter toggle clasp
12 inches .018-inch-diameter nylon-coated flexible beading wire
Round-nose pliers
Chain-nose pliers
Crimp pliers
Flush cutters

FINISHED SIZE
7¾ inches (including clasp)

SPRiNG FLiRT

Design by Camilla Jorgensen

These are the perfect spring earrings—light, bright and full of energy. Start with a simple finding and finish these stunning earrings in a few minutes.

INSTRUCTIONS

1) Slide a crystal onto a head pin. Form a loop above crystal; trim excess wire. Repeat for each crystal and pearl.

2) Open loop on a pearl dangle. Slide onto center loop inside chandelier finding; close loop.

3) Open loops on seven crystal dangles. Attach to bottom loops of chandelier finding; close loops.

4) Open loop on an ear wire and attach to top loop of chandelier finding; close loop.

5) Repeat steps 2–4 for second earring. ●

Sources: CRYSTALLIZED™ - Swarovski Elements crystals from Frabels Inc.; sterling silver findings, chandelier findings and ear wires from Fire Mountain Gems and Beads.

MATERIALS
14 (4mm) CRYSTALLIZED™ - Swarovski Elements bicone crystals
2 (6–7mm) freshwater pearls
16 (1-inch) sterling silver head pins
2 (40mm) sterling silver chandelier findings with 8 holes
2 sterling silver ear wires with drop
Round-nose pliers
Flat-nose pliers
Flush cutters

FINISHED SIZE
2 inches long

intermediate

BLOSSOM NECKLACE

Design by Melanie Brooks Lukacs, courtesy of Earthenwood Studio

*Like a picture perfect summertime day, this blossoming flower necklace
helps you celebrate the new growth of the year!*

INSTRUCTIONS

1) Open a connector ring and slide onto daisy pendant. Close connector. Set aside.

2) Cut an 8-inch length of beading wire. String a crimp tube onto beading wire 2 inches from end. String following seed beads: 11/0, 8/0, 11/0, 8/0, 11/0, 8/0, two 11/0, 8/0, 11/0, 8/0, 11/0, 8/0 and 11/0. Thread short wire tail back through crimp tube forming a beaded loop. Use crimp pliers to flatten and fold crimp tube. Trim short wire up next to crimp. Attach a crimp cover over crimp tube using chain-nose pliers to close cover.

3) String five olive rondelles, daisy pendant, five olive rondelles, silver saucer, orange pumpkin, silver saucer, yellow pumpkin, silver saucer, orange pumpkin, silver saucer and 10 olive rondelles.

4) String a crimp tube and complete a beaded loop in the same manner as in step 2.

5) Use a connector ring to attach button to center of previous beaded loop. Repeat to attach floral link to center of opposite beaded loop. Repeat to attach "blossom" link to other side of floral link.

6) Repeat step 2 with 20-inch beading wire.

7) String 88 olive rondelles, silver saucer, orange pumpkin, silver saucer and 8/0 seed bead.

Continued on page 35

MATERIALS
30mm orange stained glass daisy pendant
20mm dark orange stained glass floral link
12 x 10mm porcelain pumpkin beads: 3 orange, 1 yellow
35 x 10mm orange "blossom" porcelain message link
108 (6 x 3mm) olive fiber-optic rondelles
6 (6mm) sterling silver saucer beads
5 (4 x 6mm) sterling silver connector rings
Seed beads: 32 (8/0) lime color-lined, 38 (11/0) lime
18mm yellow daisy button
4 (2 x 2mm) sterling silver crimp tubes
4 (3mm) sterling silver crimp covers
28 inches .018-inch-diameter nylon-coated flexible beading wire
Chain-nose pliers
Crimp pliers
Wire cutters

FINISHED SIZE
20½ inches (including clasp)

easy

FANFARE FOR TULiPS

Design by Barb Switzer

Spring's first tulips appear with a bright splash of vibrant colors.
Capture the bright energy of blooming flowers on your wrist.

INSTRUCTIONS

1) String a crimp bead, daisy spacer, flower bead, daisy spacer and a seed bead 1 inch from one end of wire. Thread short wire tail back through daisy spacer, flower bead, daisy spacer and crimp bead. Use crimp pliers to flatten and fold crimp bead.

2) String a seed bead and a green rondelle.

3) String a daisy spacer, amethyst round, daisy spacer, red rondelle, daisy spacer, amethyst round, daisy spacer and a green rondelle. Repeat four more times, skipping the green rondelle on the last repeat and ending with a daisy spacer.

4) String a crimp bead and 16 seed beads. Thread wire back through crimp bead forming a beaded loop making sure beads are snug but not too tight. Flatten and fold crimp bead. Trim excess wire. ●

Sources: Flower bead from Michele Goldstein; rondelles from Talisman Associates Inc.; seed beads, daisy spacers, crimp beads and beading wire from Fusion Beads.

MATERIALS
Flat handmade glass flower bead
10 (10mm) amethyst round beads
6 x 8mm faceted glass rondelles:
    5 green, 5 red
18 (8/0) purple seed beads
22 (4mm) silver daisy spacers
2 (1.3mm) silver crimp beads

9 inches .019-inch-diameter
    nylon-coated flexible
    beading wire
Crimp pliers
Wire cutters

FINISHED SIZE
8¼ inches (including clasp)

CRYSTALS & DAiSiES

Design by Carole Rodgers

Don't be afraid to let your wire show! Sterling-plated beading wire wraps around crystals like a delicate climbing vine.

INSTRUCTIONS

1) String a crimp bead onto wire ½ inch from one end. Thread short wire tail through a loop on one half of clasp and back through crimp bead. Use crimp pliers to flatten and fold crimp bead.

2) String a 3mm silver bead and another crimp bead. Flatten and fold crimp bead.

3) String a 3mm silver bead and a 2mm silver bead.

4) String a teal AB crystal. Thread wire back through crystal in same direction making a loop (Fig. 1). Thread wire back through crystal again making a second loop (Fig. 2).

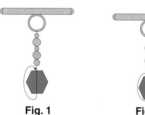

| Fig. 1 | Fig. 2 |

5) String a 2mm silver bead, 3mm silver bead and a 2mm silver bead.

6) Repeat steps 4 and 5 five more times. Repeat step 4.

7) String a 2mm silver bead, teal daisy and a 2mm silver bead.

8) Repeat step 4.

9) Repeat steps 7 and 8 ten more times. Repeat step 7.

10) Repeat steps 4 and 5 six times. Repeat step 4.

11) String a 2mm silver bead, 3mm silver bead, crimp bead, 3mm silver bead and a crimp bead.

12) Thread wire through loop on remaining half of clasp and back through last set of beads in step.

13) Flatten and fold crimp beads. Trim excess wire. ●

Sources: Daisy beads from Cousin Corp. of America; metal beads from Jay's of Tucson; toggle clasp from Crafts Etc!; crimp beads and beading wire from Beadalon.

MATERIALS

12 (15 x 5mm) teal daisy beads
25 (6mm) teal AB bicone crystals
Silver-plated round metal beads:
    50 (2mm), 16 (3mm)
4 (2mm) silver crimp beads
Silver daisy toggle clasp
60 inches .015-inch-diameter
    19-strand nylon-coated flexible
    sterling-plated beading wire
Crimp pliers
Wire cutters

FINISHED SIZE

21 inches (including clasp)

RAiNBOW RAYS

Design by Camilla Jorgenson

You'll need to make more than one of these enchanting and easy bracelets. Mix shapes and colors into a sparkly rainbow bouquet.

INSTRUCTIONS

1) Slide a crystal onto head pin; form a loop. Trim excess wire. Open 6mm jump ring and slide on beaded dangle; close ring. Set aside.

2) String a crimp tube onto beading wire 1 inch from end. Insert short wire tail through a Wire Guardian and back through crimp tube. Use crimp pliers to flatten crimp tube. Cover crimp tube with crimp cover.

3) Beginning and ending with a sterling silver round bead, string all crystals and silver round beads alternating between the two.

4) String a crimp tube. Thread wire through a Wire Guardian and back through crimp tube and a few crystals. Flatten crimp tube. Trim excess wire. Cover crimp tube with crimp cover.

5) Open 6mm jump ring and attach to one end of bracelet; close ring.

6) Open 4mm jump ring and attach to loop on clasp and opposite end of bracelet. Close ring. ●

Source: CRYSTALLIZED™ - Swarovski Elements crystals and sterling silver findings from Frabels Inc.

MATERIALS
19–25 (6–12mm) CRYSTALLIZED™ - Swarovski Elements crystals in assorted shapes, sizes and colors
19–26 (2mm) sterling silver round beads
2 (1.3mm) silver crimp tubes
2 sterling silver crimp covers
12mm sterling silver head pin
Sterling silver jump rings:
   1 (4mm), 1 (6mm)
2 sterling silver Wire Guardians
10mm sterling silver lobster-claw clasp
11 inches .019-inch-diameter nylon-coated flexible beading wire
Round-nose pliers
Flat-nose pliers
Crimp pliers
Wire cutters

FINISHED SIZE
7½ inches (including clasp)

easy

PAPAYA FLOWER

Design by Fernando Dasilva

Delicate petal filigree, lustrous pearls, incredible fruity padparadscha crystals and a sophisticated off-set Venetian pebble will transport you to the tropics.

INSTRUCTIONS

Pendant

1) Glue bicone crystal inside center of filigree rose. Set aside to dry.

2) Cut five 4-inch lengths of dark pink wire.

3) String a 4mm round crystal onto a 4-inch pink wire; center crystal on wire. Insert wire ends through a flower petal on filigree rose from front to back. Cross wires over each other on back of flower and back through opposite holes. Pass wires through crystal in opposite directions. Trim one wire flush with crystal hole. Wrap other wire around base of crystal. Trim excess wire.

4) Repeat step 3 with remaining four lengths of dark pink wire.

5) For beaded bail, pass a 3-inch length of beading wire through center top hole on one of the flower petals.

6) String a dark pink seed bead and a gold seed bead. Repeat five more times. String one more gold seed bead and a .8mm crimp tube. Insert opposite wire end through crimp tube in opposite direction (Fig. 1). Pull to tighten. Use crimp pliers to flatten and fold crimp tube. Trim excess wire. Set pendant aside.

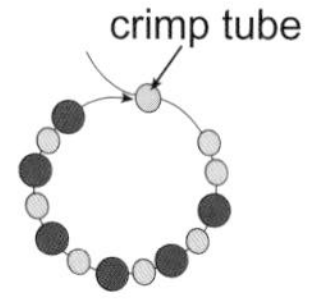

crimp tube

Fig. 1

MATERIALS
Medium white filigree rose
CRYSTALLIZED™ - Swarovski
  Elements crystals: 11 (8mm)
  padparadscha AB round,
  13 (4mm) padparadscha round,
  1 (6mm) padparadscha bicone
31 (12mm) white cultured
  freshwater coin pearls
14 (13 x 16mm) pink oval beads
19 x 14mm dark pink dichroic
  pebble Venetian bead
Seed beads: 7 (12/0) gold,
  6 (15/0) dark pink
40 sterling silver spacer beads
113 (2mm) white oval
  Bead Bumpers
Silver-plated crimp tubes:
  4 (1.5mm), 1 (.8mm)

4 silver-plated crimp covers
4 silver-plated Wire Guardians
Sterling silver square toggle
  clasp with 3 loops
20 inches 26-gauge dark
  pink wire
43 inches .018-inch-diameter
  19-strand nylon-coated
  flexible beading wire
Round-nose pliers
Chain-nose pliers
Crimp pliers
Flush cutters
Jewelry glue

FINISHED SIZE
18 inches (including clasp)

Necklace

1) Cut a 20-inch length of beading wire. String a 1.5mm crimp tube onto wire 1 inch from end. Insert short wire tail through a Wire Guardian, top loop of one half of clasp and back through crimp tube. Flatten and fold crimp tube. Trim short wire tail. Cover crimp tube with crimp cover.

2) String the following: two Bead Bumpers, silver spacer, pink oval, silver spacer, 4mm round crystal, silver spacer and a pink oval.

3) String a silver spacer, 8mm round crystal, silver spacer and a pink oval. Repeat five more times.

4) String a silver spacer, 8mm round crystal, silver spacer, pearl, Venetian bead and pink oval.

5) Repeat beading sequence from step 3 four times.

6) String a silver spacer, 4mm round crystal, silver spacer, pink oval, silver spacer and two Bead Bumpers.

7) String a 1.5mm crimp tube. Insert wire through a Wire Guardian, top loop of toggle bar and back through crimp tube. Flatten and fold crimp tube. Trim excess wire. Cover crimp tube with crimp cover.

8) Repeat step 1 to attach remaining 20-inch wire to bottom loop of clasp.

9) String two Bead Bumpers.

10) String a silver spacer, 4mm round crystal and a silver spacer.

11) String six white pearls, stringing three Bead Bumpers before and after each pearl.

12) Repeat steps 10 and 11. Repeat step 10.

13) Repeat step 11, stringing pendant after third pearl. *Note: Pendant will sit on top of Bead Bumpers.*

14) Repeat steps 10 and 11 two times. Repeat steps 10 and 9.

15) String a 1.5mm crimp tube. Insert wire through a Wire Guardian, bottom loop of clasp and back through crimp tube. Flatten and fold crimp tube. Trim excess wire. Cover crimp tube with crimp cover. ●

Sources: Crystals from CRYSTALLIZED™ - Swarovski Elements; Venetian bead from VenetianBeadShop.com; coin pearls from Shogun Trading Co. Inc.; glass beads from Wraps Stones & Things; seed beads from Great Craft Works; spacers and toggle clasp from John Bead Corp.; dark pink wire, beading wire, Wire Guardians, Bead Bumpers, crimp tubes and crimp covers from Beadalon.

LUCK OF THE iRiSH

Continued from page 18

9mm white pearl and one olive crystal. String a dark green pearl, bronze round bead, two 3mm olivine round beads, pendant, bronze round bead and a dark green pearl.

7) String 3½ inches of prehnite chips randomly inserting the following: two 9mm white pearls, olive crystal and one dark green pearl. String a dark green pearl, bronze round bead and three 3mm olivine round beads.

8) Cut a 20-inch length of gold wire. Form half of a wrapped loop at one end of wire making loop same size as loop at end of bronze wire. Hold both loops together and finish wrapping gold wire around wraps of bronze wire wrapping four to five times to secure.

9) Randomly string 3mm olivine round beads, pistachio pearls, 3mm white pearls,

6mm olivine round beads and bronze round beads, wrapping gold wire loosely around bronze strand while stringing. Continue stringing and wrapping until you near end of wire. Repeat step 8 with wire end. Trim excess wire.

10) Open link at end of chain and attach to wrapped loop; close link. Open a jump ring and slide on another jump ring; attach to opposite end of chain. Close ring. Add two more jump rings to jump-ring chain. Attach toggle bar to last jump ring.

11) Open a jump ring and slide on another jump ring; attach to opposite end of necklace. Close ring. Attach toggle round to last jump ring. ●

Sources: Jade teardrop from South Sun Products Inc.; prehnite chips, pearls, Czech glass beads and crystals from Fire Mountain Gems and Beads; brass pendant, toggle clasp, jump rings and wire from Brass Bouquet; brass chain from Michaels Stores Inc.

BLOSSOM NECKLACE

Continued from page 24

8) String a crimp tube. Beginning and ending with an 11/0 seed bead, string 14 (11/0) seed beads and 13 (8/0) seed beads alternating between the two. Insert wire back through crimp tube and several other beads. Flatten and fold crimp tube. Trim excess wire. Attach a crimp cover over crimp tube.

9) Use a connector ring to attach beaded loop from step 6 to other side of "blossom" link to complete necklace. ●

Sources: Porcelain beads and message link from Earthenwood Studio; stained glass pendant and floral link from Lily Studios; fiber-optic rondelles from Rings & Things; connector rings from Rio Grande; sterling silver beads, seed beads, button, findings and beading wire from Fusion Beads.

SUMMER

Bright, punchy colors throw open the windows to warm breezes and the smell of freshly cut grass. Celebrate Memorial Day, Independence Day and the warmest weather of the year.

beginner

PROMiSED DREAM

Designs by Rupa Balachandar

Brighten up a white shirt and jeans or express your patriotism with carved turquoise, rock crystal, coral, hematite, Bali silver and lapis beads.

INSTRUCTIONS

Necklace

1) String a crimp bead onto wire 1½ inches from one end. Thread short wire tail through a Wire Guardian and one half of clasp; insert short wire back through crimp bead. Use crimp pliers to flatten crimp bead.

2) String the following: sterling silver round, bead cap, 6mm coral, hematite, daisy spacer, two crystal rounds, pearl, daisy spacer, hematite, 6mm coral, crown spacer, turquoise, crown spacer, 6mm coral, sterling silver round, silver Bali-style bead, sterling silver round and coral nugget.

3) String the following: sterling silver round, silver Bali-style bead, sterling silver round, hematite, daisy spacer, crackled quartz, daisy spacer, hematite, 6mm coral, daisy spacer, 6mm coral, silver drum, 6mm coral, daisy spacer, 6mm coral, daisy spacer, sodalite, crown spacer and turquoise.

4) String the following: crown spacer, pearl, daisy spacer, lapis, sterling silver round, silver Bali-style and sterling silver round.

5) String a coral nugget.

6) Repeat steps 2–4 in reverse to complete other half of necklace.

7) String a crimp bead. Thread wire through a Wire Guardian, remaining half of clasp and back through crimp bead. Flatten crimp bead. Trim excess wire.

Earrings

1) Slide a 4mm coral, daisy spacer, hematite, bead cap and a sterling silver round onto a head pin. Form a wrapped loop above beads. Trim excess wire. Repeat once.

2) Open loops on ear wires and slide on beaded dangles; close loops. ●

Source: Beads and findings from RupaB Designs.

MATERIALS

Coral round beads: 14 (6mm), 2 (4mm)
10 (6mm) hematite round beads
4 (8mm) crystal round beads
4 (8 x 5mm) white freshwater rice pearls
4 (15mm) carved turquoise round beads
3 (25 x 20mm) coral nugget beads
2 (12mm) crackled quartz round beads
2 (10 x 5mm) sodalite heishi beads
2 (8mm) lapis round beads
16 (3mm) sterling silver round beads
18 (5mm) silver daisy spacers
8 (6 x 3mm) silver crown spacers
6 (5mm) silver Bali-style beads
2 (10 x 12mm) silver Bali-style drum beads
4 (5mm) silver Bali-style bead caps
2 (2-inch) silver head pins
2 silver Wire Guardians
2 (2mm) silver crimp beads
2 silver ear wires
Silver Bali-style hook-and-eye clasp
25 inches .016-inch-diameter or .015-inch-diameter nylon-coated flexible beading wire
Flat-nose pliers
Chain-nose pliers
Crimp pliers
Wire cutters

FINISHED SIZES

Necklace
21¾ inches (including clasp)
Earrings
1½ inches long

SONG OF SUMMER

Design by Andrew Thornton

Carrying both feather and leaf alike, a breeze whistles through a hot summer day. This necklace with its cool color palette, beachy components and copper wire, captures the song of summer.

INSTRUCTIONS

1) Cut a 1½-inch length of copper wire. Form a wrapped loop at one end with four coils. Trim short wire end if needed. String a white coral rondelle. Form another wrapped loop with four coils creating a white coral link. Trim excess wire.

2) Cut a 1½-inch length of copper wire. Form a wrapped loop at one end with four coils, attaching loop to wrapped loop on white coral link before wrapping. String a white coral rondelle. Form a wrapped loop with four coils. Trim excess wire.

3) Repeat step 2 three more times attaching each link to previous white coral link. This creates a white coral link chain. Make sure loops in each link are even and facing same direction. If loops are askew, chain will roll and not lay flat. Set aside.

4) In the same manner, create a turquoise nugget link chain consisting of 13 turquoise nugget links. **Note:** *Attach last wrapped loop to one half of clasp before wrapping.*

5) Cut a 2-inch length of copper wire. Form a wrapped loop with four coils at one end, attaching loop to ceramic leaf before wrapping. String bird bead. Form another wrapped loop with four coils, attaching loop to bottom loops on white coral and turquoise nugget chains before wrapping.

6) String a crimp tube onto beading wire ½ inch from one end. Insert short wire tail through top loop on white coral link chain and back through crimp tube. Use crimp pliers to flatten and fold crimp tube. Attach crimp cover on top of crimp tube.

Continued on page 62

MATERIALS

25 x 42mm blue ceramic leaf
11 x 26mm fine pewter bird bead
5 (10 x 7mm) white
  coral rondelles
13 (9 x 10mm) turquoise nuggets
20 (6 x 7mm) light blue pearls
16mm polymer clay round bead
15 x 22mm pewter
  magnetic clasp
2 (2 x 2mm) gold-filled
  crimp tubes
2 (4mm) silver crimp tube covers

8 inches .019-inch-diameter
  nylon-coated flexible
  beading wire
29 inches 22-gauge half-hard
  copper wire
Round-nose pliers
Chain-nose pliers
Crimp pliers
Wire cutters

FINISHED SIZE

21 inches (including clasp),
  with a 2½-inch droplet

beginner

SEA OF CORTEZ

Design by Brenda Morris Jarrett

I didn't know how to use these mother-of-pearl buttons until I went to visit my brother's home on Mexico's Sea of Cortez. The gorgeous browns of the sand, shells and earth made me choose all natural beads. Can you feel the wet sand beneath your bare feet as you walk along the shore picking up shells?

INSTRUCTIONS

1) Beginning on front of button, insert 2 inches of beading wire through one buttonhole. String three pearls onto long wire. Insert long wire down through second hole.

2) String two pearls and a bamboo tube onto each wire on back of button. String a crimp bead onto long wire. Insert short wire tail through crimp bead and pull wire to tighten. Use crimp pliers to flatten and fold crimp bead.

3) String a mother-of-pearl round bead and a wooden elliptical bead. Repeat four more times.

4) String three mother-of-pearl nuggets and 10 penshell heishi beads. Repeat once.

5) String one crimp bead, wooden bean, crimp bead and a bamboo tube. Repeat two more times. String a crimp bead, wooden bean and a crimp bead.

6) String three mother-of-pearl round beads, seven tiger's-eye chips, three mother-of-pearl round beads and three wooden elliptical beads.

7) String five penshell heishi beads and two mother-of-pearl nuggets. Repeat once.

8) String four tiger's-eye chips and two mother-of-pearl nuggets. Repeat once.

Continued on page 62

MATERIALS
1-inch shell button
31 (2–2.5mm) white button pearls
11 (6mm) mother-of-pearl round beads
14 mother-of-pearl nuggets
4 wooden bean-shaped beads
8 wooden elliptical beads
7 bamboo tubes
15 tiger's-eye chips
30 penshell heishi beads
15 (1.3mm) copper crimp beads
24 inches .018-inch-diameter 49-strand nylon-coated flexible beading wire
Crimp pliers
Wire cutters

FINISHED SIZE
19 inches (including clasp)

FiESTA FLORES

Design by Brenda Morris Jarrett

These bright and colorful lampwork flower beads by Lisa Hanna are a party in themselves. Put them on your wrist and see how a festival starts!

INSTRUCTIONS

1) Open a twist jump ring and slide it onto a flower button. Slide jump ring onto center link of chain. Close ring.

2) Skip seven links and attach another flower button in the same manner. Repeat on other side of first flower button.

3) In the same manner, attach flower buttons to both sides of chain 3 links from each end.

4) Slide a saucer bead and a flower bead onto a head pin. Skip three links from center flower button and slide beaded head pin through link. Form a small loop at end of head pin and roll into a spiral securing flower bead to chain. Repeat on other side of center flower button.

5) In the same manner, attach beaded head pins to each side of chain three links from end flower buttons.

6) Open a jump ring and slide it onto flower half of clasp; slide jump ring onto one end of chain. Close ring. Open another jump ring and slide it through flower half of clasp, first jump ring and end of chain. Close ring.

7) Attach a jump ring to opposite end of bracelet. Open another jump ring and slide it through previous jump ring and end link of chain; close ring. Repeat step 6 to attach toggle bar to previous jump rings. ●

Sources: Lampwork beads from The LH Bead Gallery; saucer beads from Artbeads.com; twist jump rings from Rio Grande; head pins, jump rings and chain from Fire Mountain Gems and Beads; flower toggle clasp from Crafts Etc!

MATERIALS

4 multicolored lampwork flower beads with center hole
5 multicolored lampwork flower button beads
4 (3.3mm) sterling silver saucer beads
4 (3-inch) sterling silver head pins
5 (8mm) sterling silver twist jump rings
6 (5.3mm) sterling silver jump rings
Sterling silver flower toggle clasp
7 inches (35 links) 5.7mm sterling silver heavy cable chain
Round-nose pliers
Needle-nose pliers
Wire cutters

FINISHED SIZE

8¼ inches (including clasp)

intermediate

RED HOT SUMMER SiZZLERS

Design by Andrew Thornton

Nothing embodies summer like an outdoor picnic with a barbeque grill filled with red-hot coals. Full of movement and bright red color, these earrings attempt to capture some of that sizzling fun under the sun.

INSTRUCTIONS

1) Cut a 1½-inch length of wire. Form a wrapped loop at one end, attaching loop to bottom of ear wire before wrapping.

2) String a crystal. Form another wrapped loop. Trim excess wire.

3) Cut a 2-inch length of wire. Form a wrapped loop at one end, attaching loop to previous wrapped loop.

4) String a 20 x 9.5mm red teardrop with point facing down. Form another wrapped loop. Trim excess wire.

5) Cut a 1½-inch length of wire. Thread wire through a 5 x 6mm red teardrop, centering bead on wire. Bring wire ends above bead and wrap one wire around other wire just above bead securing bead to wire. Form other end of wire into a wrapped loop, attaching loop to previous wrapped loop before wrapping. Trim excess wire.

6) Repeat steps 1–5 to make second earring. ●

Sources: Czech glass beads from Talisman Associates Inc.; bicone crystals and wire from Fusion Beads; gunmetal ear wires from Saki Silver.

MATERIALS
2 (6mm) siam CRYSTALLIZED™-
    Swarovski Elements
    bicone crystals
Red Czech glass teardrop
    beads: 2 (20 x 9.5mm)
    vertically-drilled,
    2 (5 x 6mm) top-drilled
2 (20x 38mm) gunmetal almond-
    shaped ear wires
10 inches 24-gauge dead-soft
    sterling silver wire
Round-nose pliers
Chain-nose pliers
Flush cutters

FINISHED SIZE
3½ inches long

SUNDOG

Design by Erin Strother

Pastel and earth tones, glass, stone and silver are as soothing as a long nap on a warm afternoon.

INSTRUCTIONS

1) Using both pairs of chain-nose pliers, open a 4mm jump ring and attach it to one 3mm jump ring and one half of clasp. Close ring.

2) String a crimp tube ½ inch from one end of beading wire. Insert short wire tail through 3mm jump ring from step 1 and back through crimp tube. Use crimp pliers to flatten and fold crimp tube.

3) String lavender seed bead, olive round, aquamarine nugget, silver triangle, aventurine rondelle, Ching-Hai jade rondelle and 12 aventurine rondelles.

4) String a silver spacer, two Ching-Hai jade rondelles, olive jade rectangle, aventurine rondelle and a 5 x 4mm silver bead.

5) String an aquamarine nugget and a silver triangle. Repeat two more times.

6) String an aquamarine nugget, silver spacer, two aventurine rondelles, olive jade rectangle, Ching-Hai jade rondelle, 10 x 5mm silver bead and olive round.

7) String Kazuri bead.

8) Repeat steps 3–6 in reverse to string remaining half of necklace.

9) Repeat step 1 with other half of clasp. String crimp tube onto wire. Insert wire through 3mm jump ring and back through crimp tube and several other beads. Flatten and fold crimp tube. Trim excess wire. ●

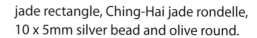

Sources: Kazuri bead from Kazuri West; olive jade beads, rondelles, aquamarine nuggets, seed beads and Czech glass beads from Fire Mountain Gems and Beads; sterling silver beads, findings and clasp from Gemshow-Online Jewelry Supply.

MATERIALS

Aqua/olive/tan striped Kazuri tube bead
10 (12 x 8mm) aquamarine nuggets
4 (12 x 8mm) olive jade rectangle beads
8mm rondelles: 8 Ching Hai "jade," 32 red aventurine
4 (6mm) olivine Czech glass faceted round beads
2 (6/0) matte lavender seed beads
Sterling silver Bali-style beads: 2 (10 x 5mm), 2 (5 x 4mm)
4 (7mm) sterling silver spacer beads
8 (2mm) sterling silver Hill Tribe triangle beads
Sterling silver jump rings: 2 (3mm) closed, 2 (4mm)
2 (2mm) sterling silver crimp tubes
Sterling silver Bali-style S clasp
19 inches .018-inch-diameter nylon-coated flexible beading wire
2 pairs of chain-nose pliers
Crimp pliers
Flush cutters

FINISHED SIZE

17¼ inches (including clasp)

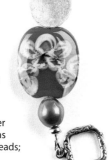

CARiBBEAN FANCY

Design by Lisa Liddy

These handmade lampwork beads from artist Verna Hedgecoth's reminded me of the colors and patterns in a tropical sarong. I added freshwater pearls and Hill Tribe silver because they go with everything.

INSTRUCTIONS

1) String a crimp tube and a Wire Guardian onto beading wire 1 inch from end. Insert short wire tail through loop on one half of clasp and back through crimp tube. Use crimp pliers to flatten and fold crimp tube.

2) String beads as follows: spacer, pearl, lampwork bead, silver coin, lampwork bead and pearl.

3) String focal square. Repeat step 2 in reverse.

4) String a crimp tube and a Wire Guardian. Insert wire through loop on other half of clasp and back through crimp tube. Flatten and fold crimp tube. Trim excess wire. ●

Sources: Lampwork beads from Bead Addicts; silver beads and toggle clasp from Somerset Silver Inc.; pearls from Majestic Pearl Inc.; Wire Guardians and crimp tubes from Fire Mountain Gems and Beads; beading wire from Soft Flex Co.

MATERIALS

4 (18 x 20mm) tropical blue floral lampwork crunch-style beads
4 (8–10mm) deep burgundy freshwater pearls
2 (15mm) silver Hill Tribe coin beads
28 x 28 x 14mm silver Hill Tribe focal square
2 (4–5mm) sterling silver spacers
2 (2mm) sterling silver crimp tubes
2 sterling silver Wire Guardians
15mm silver Hill Tribe toggle clasp
10 inches .019-inch-diameter 49-strand nylon-coated flexible beading wire
Round-nose pliers
Chain-nose pliers
Crimp pliers
Flush cutters

FINISHED SIZE

8¾ inches (including clasp)

SEA TREASURE

Design by Liz Revit

From the depths of the sea to sun-drenched sands, this necklace is perfect for anyone who loves the ocean. Using Joan Miller's porcelain mermaid pendant as the focal piece, this necklace captures all that reminds one of those endless summer days.

Project note: *Use both pairs of chain-nose pliers to open jump rings; use split-ring pliers to open split ring.*

INSTRUCTIONS

1) String a crimp tube onto wire ½ inch from one end. Thread short wire tail through jump ring attached to clasp and back through crimp tube. Use crimp pliers to flatten and fold crimp tube. Trim short wire tail close to crimp tube.

2) String a random mix of turquoise chips, amethyst chips, seashell beads, seed beads, pewter spacers and glass cathedral beads until beaded section measures 6½ inches. End pattern with a cathedral glass bead.

3) For center section, string one 11/0 seed bead, 8/0 seed bead, pewter spacer, 8/0 seed bead, pewter spacer and an 8/0 seed bead.

4) String end link of ¾-inch chain. Repeat step 3 in reverse.

5) Beginning with a cathedral glass bead, repeat beading pattern from step 2.

6) String a crimp tube. Thread wire through split ring and back through crimp tube. Flatten and fold crimp tube. Trim excess wire.

Continued on page 62

MATERIALS

1¼-inch-diameter porcelain mermaid pendant
25 pewter daisy spacers
Seed beads: 32 (11/0) light topaz AB, 40 (8/0) light caramel Ceylon
Cathedral glass beads: 6 aqua, 6 green
21 Chinese turquoise chips
17 amethyst chips
13 small drilled seashell beads
CRYSTALLIZED™ - Swarovski Elements bicone crystals:
  1 (6mm) mint alabaster,
  1 (4mm) mint alabaster,
  1 (6mm) light Colorado topaz,
  1 (4mm) light Colorado topaz,
  1 (6mm) Pacific opal,
  1 (4mm) Pacific opal
2 (1.3mm) silver crimp tubes
6 (1½-inch) 24-gauge sterling silver head pins
2 (7mm) silver-plated jump rings
6mm sterling silver split ring
Silver-plated oval-link chain:
  1 (¾-inch) length,
  1 (2½-inch) length
10 x 4mm sterling silver lobster-claw clasp with jump ring
17 inches .018-inch-diameter 49-strand nylon-coated flexible beading wire
Round-nose pliers
2 pairs of chain-nose pliers
Crimp pliers
Split-ring pliers
Wire cutters

FINISHED SIZE

15¼ inches (including clasp), plus a 2½-inch extender chain

beginner

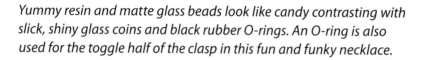

FRUiT PUNCH

Design by Erin Strother

Yummy resin and matte glass beads look like candy contrasting with slick, shiny glass coins and black rubber O-rings. An O-ring is also used for the toggle half of the clasp in this fun and funky necklace.

INSTRUCTIONS

1) Open a jump ring and slide it onto loop on toggle bar and two 5mm O-rings. Close ring. Open another jump ring and slide it through previous two O-rings. Slide two more 5mm O-rings onto second jump ring. Close ring.

2) Cut a 2-inch length of wire. Form a loop at one end. String an orange seed bead, light blue rondelle, pink resin bicone and a black rondelle.

3) Form a loop. Trim excess wire. Open first loop and slide it through last set of O-rings. Close loop. Open opposite loop and slide on two 5mm O-rings; close loop. Open a jump ring and slide it onto last set of O-rings. Slide a 12mm O-ring onto jump ring. Close ring. Attach another jump ring to other side of 12mm O-ring. Slide two 5mm O-rings onto jump ring. Close ring.

4) Cut a 3-inch length of wire and form a loop at one end. String an orange seed bead, light blue rondelle, lime green saucer, amethyst rondelle, orange resin rectangle, black rondelle, olivine coin, amethyst rondelle and a light blue rondelle.

5) Repeat step 3.

6) Cut a 2¼-inch length of wire and form a loop at one end. String a black rondelle, pink resin rectangle, black rondelle and a light blue rondelle.

7) Repeat step 3.

8) Cut a 2-inch length of wire and form a loop at one end. String an orange seed bead, amethyst rondelle, olivine coin and a light blue rondelle.

9) Repeat step 3.

Continued on page 63

MATERIALS

Resin beads: 2 (25 x 13mm) pink rectangles, 1 (15 x 13mm) orange teardrop, 1 (10 x 8mm) orange 5-sided rectangle, 1 (18 x 12mm) pink bicone
2 (14.5mm) olivine Czech pressed glass coin beads
Matte lime green glass beads: 1 (5 x 10mm) saucer, 1 (10 x 8mm) cylinder, 1 (10mm) bicone
6mm glass rondelles: 10 black, 6 amethyst, 7 light blue
Seed beads: 6 (6/0) orange, 1 (10/0) lime green

Black rubber O-rings: 7 (12mm), 30 (5mm)
15 (7mm) 18-gauge aluminum jump rings
¾-inch silver head pin
Silver toggle bar
16¾ inches 18-gauge silver craft wire
Round-nose pliers
Chain-nose pliers
Flush cutters

FINISHED SIZE

18⅜ inches (including clasp)

beginner

PiNK PADDLES

Design by Carole Rodgers

These pink paddle-shaped beads are actually magenta-dyed jade beads and vary greatly in size. Strung together, paddle shapes look similar to a Hawaiian lei.

INSTRUCTIONS

1) String a crimp tube onto beading wire 1 inch from end. Insert short wire through narrow end of a bead cap and then through wide end of another bead cap. String a crimp tube. Insert wire through round end of clasp and back through both crimp tubes and bead caps. Use crimp pliers to flatten crimp tubes.

2) String 15 paddle-shaped beads.

3) Thread wire through narrow end of a bead cap, a Bali bead and wide end of a bead cap.

4) Repeat steps 2 and 3 four more times. Repeat step 2.

5) Attach split ring to toggle bar.

6) String a crimp tube. Thread wire through narrow end of a bead cap and then through wide end of another bead cap. String a crimp tube.

7) Insert wire through split ring and back through both crimp tubes and bead caps. Flatten crimp tubes. Trim excess wire. ●

Sources: Paddle-shaped beads from CR Enterprises; Bali-style beads and bead caps from Village Originals Inc.; findings and beading wire from Beadalon.

MATERIALS

16-inch strand 5 x 15mm magenta-dyed paddle-shaped beads
5 (10 x 14mm) silver Bali-style beads
14 (4 x 6mm) silver Bali-style bead caps
5mm silver split ring
4 (2mm) silver crimp tubes
15mm silver Bali-style toggle clasp
24 inches .018-inch-diameter 19-strand nylon-coated flexible beading wire
Crimping pliers
Chain-nose pliers
Split-ring pliers
Wire cutters

FINISHED SIZE

19½ inches (including clasp)

FLOWER SET

Designs by Jennifer Heynen, courtesy of Jangles

Joyous, bright ceramic flowers are the focus of this set. So simple, you could make the whole set in a single evening!

Project note: *Memory wire is hard to cut and will damage regular wire cutters. Always use memory wire shears to cut wire coils.*

INSTRUCTIONS

Necklace

1) String a crimp bead onto one length of beading wire ½ inch from end. Insert short wire tail through one half of clasp and back through crimp bead. Use crimp pliers to flatten crimp bead.

2) String 8½ inches of seed beads, followed by flower pendant and 8½ more inches of seed beads.

3) String a crimp bead. Insert wire through other half of clasp and back through crimp bead. Use crimp pliers to flatten crimp bead and trim excess wire.

4) Repeat step 1 to attach second length of beading wire to one half of clasp.

5) String 8½ inches of bead mix. If desired, wrap strand around seed bead strand a couple of times. Thread wire through flower pendant. String 8½ inches of bead mix. If desired, twist around seed bead strand a couple of times.

6) String a crimp bead. Insert wire through remaining half of clasp and back through crimp bead. Flatten crimp bead. Trim excess wire.

Bracelet

1) Form a double loop at one end of memory wire. **Note:** *Due to the strength of the wire, forming loops of memory wire may take some time.*

2) String 2½ inches of bead mix, two seed beads, flower bead and two seed beads.

Continued on page 63

MATERIALS

Ceramic components: 1 (50mm) flower pendant, 3 small flower beads, 2 flower charms
34 inches bright glass bead mix
22 inches 6/0 red seed beads
4 (1mm) silver crimp beads
2 silver ear wires
Silver hook clasp
2 (20-inch) lengths .018-inch-diameter nylon-coated flexible beading wire
18 inches bracelet memory wire
Round-nose pliers
Crimp pliers
Wire cutters
Memory wire shears or heavy-duty wire cutters

FINISHED SIZES
Necklace
18 inches (including clasp)
Bracelet
Approximately 7½ inches (adjusts to fit most wrists)
Earrings
1¼ inches long

SEAHORSE BY THE SEASiDE

Design by Candie Cooper

Hear the waves crash on the beach each time you wear this lovely chain. Colored wire lace adds to the light beauty of a perfect summer accessory.

Project note: *Use 10mm silver jump rings throughout unless directed otherwise.*

INSTRUCTIONS

1) Knot each end of both lengths of lace ribbon. Apply a dot of epoxy on one knot; push knot into a cord end. Repeat for each knot. Let dry.

2) Slide a pearl and a crystal onto a head pin. Form a wrapped loop, attaching loop to a brass oval link before wrapping. Trim excess wire. Repeat twice, attaching second pearl dangle to other brass oval link and attaching third pearl dangle to a silver jump ring.

3) Attach a pinch bail to each lapis lazuli ring and to CZ drop.

4) Open a connector link and attach to a pinch bail connected to a lapis lazuli ring; slide link onto a silver jump ring before closing. Repeat for each lapis lazuli ring. **Note:** *Do not slide lapis lazuli rings onto jump ring with pearl dangle.*

5) In the same manner, use a connector link to attach CZ drop to silver jump ring with pearl dangle. Attach jump ring to bottom of seahorse pendant using a connector link.

6) Use connector links to attach the following: brass solid ring, silver jump ring, brass oval link, silver jump ring, brass solid ring, 16mm silver jump ring, brass solid ring, silver jump ring, brass oval link, silver jump ring and a brass solid ring. This forms center section of necklace.

7) Use a connector link to attach pendant to 16mm jump ring.

Continued on page 63

MATERIALS

3 (10mm) white coin pearls
3 (4mm) clear CRYSTALLIZED™ - Swarovski Elements round crystals
4 (14mm) lapis lazuli rings
8mm white round CZ drop
2½-inch brass seahorse pendant
20 medium brass connector links
2 (8 x 15mm) brass-colored oval links
4 (15 x 22mm) brass-colored oval textured solid rings
Silver round twist jump rings: 6 (10mm), 1 (16mm)
3 (2-inch) brass ball-ended head pins
4 silver cord ends
5 silver pinch bails
Brass lobster-claw clasp
2 (6-inch) lengths 6mm blue wire lace ribbon
Round-nose pliers
Chain-nose pliers
Flush cutters
Epoxy

FINISHED SIZE

20½ inches (including clasp), with a 4-inch droplet

SONG OF SUMMER

Continued from page 40

7) String a polymer clay bead and 20 pearls.

8) String a crimp tube. Insert wire through other half of clasp and back through crimp tube. Flatten and fold crimp tube. Trim excess wire. Attach crimp cover over crimp tube. ●

Sources: Turquoise nuggets, pearls, coral rondelles and clasp from Talisman Associates Inc.; bird bead from Green Girl Studios; ceramic leaf from Every Heart Crafts; polymer clay bead from Pam & Heather Wynn; crimp tubes and copper wire from Fusion Beads; beading wire from Soft Flex Co.

SEA OF CORTEZ

Continued from page 42

9) To form beaded loop at end of necklace, string a crimp bead, bamboo tube, crimp bead, six pearls, crimp bead, six pearls, crimp bead, six pearls, crimp bead, six pearls, crimp bead and a bamboo tube. Insert wire back through first crimp bead and several other beads. Pull wire to tighten. Flatten and fold only the first crimp bead. Trim excess wire. ●

Sources: Button, bamboo tubes, tiger's-eye chips and mother-of-pearl nuggets from Jo-Ann Stores Inc.; mother-of-pearl round beads and penshell heishi beads from Hobby Lobby Stores Inc.; wooden beads and crimp beads from Blue Moon Beads; button pearls and beading wire from Fire Mountain Gems and Beads.

SEA TREASURE

Continued from page 52

7) Attach end link of 2½-inch chain to split ring.

8) Open a jump ring and slide it through porcelain pendant; attach jump ring to end link of ¾-inch chain at center of necklace. Close ring. Repeat once. There should be two jump rings attached to pendant and chain.

9) Slide an 11/0 seed bead and a crystal onto a head pin followed by three or four other beads. Form a wrapped loop above bead, attaching loop to ¾-inch chain before wrapping. Trim excess wire.

10) Repeat step 9 five times. ●

Sources: Porcelain pendant from Joan Miller Porcelain Beads; pewter spacers from Talisman Associates Inc.; seed beads from Caravan Beads Inc.; seashell beads from Sweet Creek Inc.; cathedral glass beads and chain from Blue Moon Beads; chips, crystals, clasp and findings from Fusion Beads.

FRUiT PUNCH

Continued from page 54

10) Cut a 2½-inch length of wire and form a loop at one end. String an orange seed bead, lime green cylinder, black rondelle, light blue rondelle, amethyst rondelle, orange resin teardrop, black rondelle and amethyst rondelle.

11) Repeat steps 3 and 6. Repeat step 3.

12) Cut a 2¾-inch length of wire and form a loop at one end. String a black rondelle, lime bicone, amethyst rondelle and orange seed bead.

13) Repeat step 3 ending with 12mm O-ring.

14) Slide an orange seed bead, black rondelle and green seed bead onto head pin. Form a loop. Trim excess wire. Open loop and attach to last 12mm O-ring; close loop. ●

Sources: Resin beads from Beads and Pieces and Natural Touch Beads; coin beads, glass beads, rondelles, O-rings, seed beads, craft wire and toggle bar from Fire Mountain Gems and Beads; aluminum jump rings from The Ring Lord.

FLOWER SET

Continued from page 58

3) String 4 inches of bead mix, two seed beads, flower bead and two seed beads.

4) String 9½ inches of bead mix, adding seed beads randomly into mix. String two seed beads, flower bead and two seed beads. String 1 inch of bead mix.

5) Trim wire ½ inch past last bead. Form a double loop with wire end.

Earrings

1) Open loops on ear wires and slide on flower charms. Close loops. ●

Sources: Ceramic components from Jangles; bead mix, seed beads, beading wire and memory wire from Fire Mountain Gems and Beads.

SEAHORSE BY THE SEASiDE

Continued from page 60

8) Use connector links to attach ribbon lengths to brass solid rings at ends of center section.

9) Attach a silver jump ring to one end of necklace with a connector link. Open loop

on clasp and attach to opposite end of necklace. ●

Sources: Oval links, connector links, solid rings, twist jump rings, CZ drop, pinch bails and clasp from Beadalon; seahorse pendant from Ornamentea; wire lace ribbon from Fusion Beads.

FALL

Autumn colors are defined by two distinct qualities: bold and subtle. Like October skies, an undertone of gray rules the palette, turning summery bright orange to deep russet as leaves fall from the trees. Celebrate Labor Day, Columbus Day, Veteran's Day, Halloween and Thanksgiving as you nest indoors to escape falling temperatures.

HALLOWEEN BRACELET

Design by Jennifer Heynen, courtesy of Jangles

Celebrate whimsy and the spookiest holiday of the year with seasonal beads and findings. Ceramic pumpkins, black cat, ghost, bat and candy cane make for a sweet Halloween bracelet treat!

INSTRUCTIONS

1) Thread wire through loop on pumpkin half of clasp. Center clasp on wire. Holding wires as one, string a crimp bead and slide it down next to clasp. Use crimp pliers to flatten crimp bead.

2) Working with one wire, string four seed beads, green glass bead, four seed beads, silver round bead, ceramic bead and a silver round bead. Repeat once.

3) String four seed beads, silver round bead, ceramic bead, silver round bead, four seed beads, green glass bead, four seed beads and a silver round bead.

4) String a crimp bead. Insert wire through loop on toggle bar and back through crimp bead. Flatten crimp bead. Trim excess wire.

5) Working with other wire, string five seed beads, silver round bead, ceramic bead and a silver round bead. Repeat three more times. String five seed beads and a silver round bead.

6) Repeat step 4. ●

Sources: Ceramic beads and toggle clasp from Jangles; seed beads, Czech glass beads and beading wire from Fire Mountain Gems and Beads.

MATERIALS
7 assorted ceramic Halloween-
  themed beads
53 (6/0) black seed beads
16 (4mm) silver round beads
3 (6mm) green faceted Czech
  glass beads
3 (1mm) silver crimp beads
Ceramic pumpkin toggle clasp
20 inches .018-inch-diameter
  nylon-coated flexible
  beading wire
Crimp pliers
Wire cutters

FINISHED SIZE
8¾ inches (including clasp)

COPPER & SiLVER CHAiN

Design by Carole Rodgers

Copper always reminds me of autumn—falling leaves and crisp, clear days. There are a lot of copper findings, chain and beads available but it's hard to find all the parts and pieces which is why I combined copper with a touch of silver.

INSTRUCTIONS

1) To make pendant, slide the following onto head pin: copper spacer, silver spacer, copper teardrop (wide end first) and silver round bead. Form a wrapped loop; trim excess wire. Set aside.

2) Open links of 9mm copper chain and separate into two 6-link lengths and two 12-link lengths. Close links and set aside.

3) Open links of copper circle/oval chain and remove one 21-link length beginning and ending with ovals and two 9-link lengths beginning and ending with circle links. **Note:** *Save extra connector links.*

4) Open and attach a jump ring to lobster-claw clasp. Attach jump ring to end link of a 6-link chain from step 2. Close ring. Use an extra connector link to attach opposite end of 6-link chain to end link of a 9-link chain.

5) Continue to use extra connector links to attach the following to form necklace: 12-link chain, 21-link chain, 12-link chain, 9-link chain and 6-link chain.

6) Attach a jump ring to end link.

7) Separate silver chain into six 3-link pieces.

8) Carefully open connector links on each side of the first circle link on 21-link chain. Slide end links of one 3-link silver chain onto open connector links. Close links. The silver chain should lie across circle link.

Continued on page 90

MATERIALS
30 x 22mm copper teardrop bead
4mm copper spacer bead
6mm silver Bali-style spacer bead
3mm silver-plated round bead
3-inch silver Bali-style head pin
2 (8mm) copper jump rings
12mm copper lobster-claw clasp
Copper chain: 53 links 20mm ovals and 15mm circles with connector links, 36 (9mm) circle links
18 (5 x 3mm) silver oval chain links
Round-nose pliers
Chain-nose pliers
Flush cutters

FINISHED SIZE
24½ inches (including clasp) with a 1¾-inch pendant

beginner

iNDiAN SUMMER

Design by Suzann Wilson

The colors used in Indian Summer Bracelet remind us of when the leaves begin to change and we get that last breath of summer during the colder months.

INSTRUCTIONS

1) String a crimp bead onto wire ½ inch from one end. Thread short wire tail through loop on one half of clasp and back through crimp bead. Use crimp pliers to flatten and fold crimp bead.

2) String two spacer beads.

3) String a green leaf, spacer bead, blue leaf, spacer bead, amber leaf and a spacer bead. Repeat three more times.

4) String a green leaf and two spacer beads.

5) String a crimp bead. Thread wire through loop on other half of clasp and back through crimp bead. Flatten and fold crimp bead. Trim excess wire. ●

Sources: Glass leaves from Oriental Trading Co.; filigree spacer beads from Michaels Stores Inc.; toggle clasp from Super Time International; crimp beads and beading wire from Beadalon.

MATERIALS
Glass leaves: 5 green, 4 amber, 4 blue
16 gold filigree spacer beads
2 (1.3mm) gold crimp beads
Gold toggle clasp
10 inches .015-inch-diameter nylon-coated flexible beading wire

Crimp pliers
Wire cutters

FINISHED SIZE
7¾ inches (including clasp)

AUTUMN SKiES

Design by Andrew Thornton

Birds taking flight en masse, migrating and making their way to their winter homes, and copper, gold and rich red vistas mark the turning of the season. This necklace pays homage to the dazzling "in-between" season.

INSTRUCTIONS

1) Cut bar chain into six 1½-inch lengths and two 1-inch lengths. Cut cable chain into three 1½-inch lengths and one 1-inch length. Set aside.

2) Cut a 1-inch length of brown wire. Form a wrapped loop at one end. String a crystal copper bicone. Form another wrapped loop, creating a wire-wrapped link. Trim excess wire.

3) Cut another 1-inch length of brown wire. Form a wrapped loop at one end, attaching loop to wire-wrapped link from step 2 before wrapping. String a padparadscha satin bicone. Form a wrapped loop. Trim excess wire. Repeat eight more times, alternating crystal copper and padparadscha bicone crystals, attaching links to previous links creating a wire-wrapped link chain. **Note:** *Make sure loops in links are even and facing same direction.*

4) Repeat steps 2 and 3 to create a second wire-wrapped link chain. Invert second chain so that when both chains are placed next to each other, the pattern looks staggered.

5) Form a wrapped loop at one end of a 1½-inch length of brown wire, sliding loop onto one end of both chains from step 4 before wrapping. String crystal copper rondelle. Form another wrapped loop, attaching loop to bird half of clasp before wrapping. Trim excess wire. Set aside.

6) String a crimp tube onto beading wire ½ inch from one end; insert short wire tail

Continued on page 90

MATERIALS

35mm polymer clay pendant
20 (6mm) dark red faceted
   round pearls
3 (6mm) crystal copper
   CRYSTALLIZED™ - Swarovski
   Elements rondelles
8mm goldstone round bead
3 (9mm) golden coral
   round beads
4mm CRYSTALLIZED™ - Swarovski
   Elements bicone crystals:
   10 crystal copper,
   10 padparadscha satin
2 (1.5 x 2mm) gold-filled
   crimp tubes
2-inch copper ball-ended head pin

19 x 26mm shibuichi bird
   toggle clasp
Copper chain: 5½ inches
   2 x 2.5mm cable, 11 inches bar
28 inches 22-gauge brown
   craft wire
6½ inches .018-inch-diameter
   nylon-coated flexible
   beading wire
Round-nose pliers
Chain-nose pliers
Crimp pliers
Wire cutters

FINISHED SIZE

20½ inches (including clasp)

SAiNT LAURENT TASSEL

Design by Fernando Dasilva

Yves Saint Laurent's iconoclastic color sense and visionary attitude has transformed a simple tassel into a focal point in many of his creations. This piece features layers of inexpensive baroque pearls nested by kitschy gold-plated chain, fiery stones and CRYSTALLIZED™ elements.

INSTRUCTIONS

Tassel

1) Slide a 6mm round crystal onto a head pin. Form a wrapped loop. Trim excess wire. Repeat nine more times for a total of 10 crystal dangles.

2) In the same manner as in step 1, make 10 small pearl dangles and 10 large pearl dangles.

3) Cut ten 2½-inch pieces of chain.

4) Use chain-nose pliers to open end link of one 2½-inch chain. Slide a crystal dangle, large pearl dangle and small pearl dangle onto link. Close link. Repeat for each 2½-inch chain.

5) Use thick part of round-nose pliers to form a large half loop on one end of German-style wire. Loop needs to fit inside bead cone. Slide all chains from step 4 onto half loop. Continue to form

a wrapped loop securing chains to wire. Trim excess wire.

6) Slide straight end of wire into wide end of bead cone and out through narrow end. Form a wrapped loop above cone. Trim excess wire. Set tassel aside.

Bottom Strands

1) Cut a 14-inch piece of beading wire. String a crimp tube onto wire 1½ inches

---

MATERIALS

Crystal golden shadow
  CRYSTALLIZED™ - Swarovski
  Elements round crystals:
  34 (6mm), 1 (8mm)
Baroque copper cultured
  freshwater pearls:
  62 (7–8mm), 66 (4–5mm)
Graduated oval sunstone
  nuggets: 16 (8 x 4mm),
  12 (8 x 6mm)
17 (4mm) gold-plated
  corrugated beads
Large brass ornate bead cone
2 gold-plated 3-into-1 Victorian-
  style clasp connectors
12 gold-plated Wire Guardians
12 (2mm) satin gold oval
  Bead Bumpers
12 (1.3mm) gold-plated
  crimp tubes

12 (4mm) gold-plated sparkle
  crimp covers
8 (4mm) gold-plated jump rings
31 gold-plated head pins
5 inches gold-plated German-
  style wire
50 inches 6mm gold-plated
  rolo chain
64 inches .018-inch-diameter
  19-strand satin copper nylon-
  coated flexible beading wire
Round-nose pliers
Chain-nose pliers
Crimp pliers
Flush cutters

FINISHED SIZE

25 inches (including clasp),
  with a 1½-inch extender chain
Tassel measures 4 inches long

from end. Insert short wire tail through a Wire Guardian and back through crimp tube. Use crimp pliers to flatten and fold crimp tube. Attach a crimp cover over crimp tube.

2) String 10 large pearls.

3) String a 6mm round crystal, large sunstone nugget, 6mm round crystal, large sunstone nugget, 6mm round crystal, large sunstone nugget and a 6mm round crystal.

4) Repeat steps 2 and 3. String six large pearls.

5) String a crimp tube. Insert wire through a Wire Guardian and back through crimp tube and several other beads. Flatten and fold crimp tube. Trim excess wire. Attach a crimp cover over crimp tube.

6) Repeat steps 1–5 for second Bottom Strand.

Middle Strands

1) Cut two 2¾-inch pieces and two 2½-inch pieces of chain. Set aside.

2) Repeat step 1 of Bottom Strands with a 9-inch piece of beading wire.

3) String the following: seven small pearls, corrugated bead, 6mm round crystal and a corrugated bead.

4) String a small sunstone nugget, Bead Bumper, small sunstone nugget, Bead Bumper, small sunstone nugget, Bead Bumper and a small sunstone nugget.

5) Repeat step 3 in reverse.

6) Repeat step 5 of Bottom Strands.

7) Use chain-nose pliers to open end link of one 2¾-inch chain; attach link to loop at end of beaded strand. Close link. Repeat to attach one 2½-inch chain to opposite end of beaded strand.

8) Repeat steps 2–7 for second Middle Strand.

Top Strands

1) Cut four 2½-inch pieces of chain. Set aside.

2) Repeat steps 2–7 of Middle Strands two times to make two Top Strands, using 2½-inch chains instead of 2¾-inch chains.

Finishing

1) Use chain-nose pliers to open a single chain link and slide it onto loop at end of one Bottom Strand. Slide link onto top loop of Tassel. Close link.

2) Open one link of a two-link length of chain and slide it onto opposite end of Bottom Strand. Close link. Open a 4mm jump ring and slide it onto two-link chain and then onto bottom loop on a connector. Close ring.

3) Repeat steps 1 and 2 to add second Bottom Strand to opposite side of necklace.

4) Open end links of 2¾-inch lengths of chains on Middle Strands. Slide links onto tassel loop. Close links. In the same manner as in step 2, use 4mm jump rings to attach opposite ends of Middle Strands to middle loops on connectors.

5) Open end links of two 2½-inch chains on Top Strands. Slide links onto tassel loop. Close links. Use 4mm jump rings to attach opposite ends of Top Strands to top loops on connectors.

6) Use a 4mm jump ring to attach hook clasp onto end loop of connector. Repeat to attach a 1½-inch length of chain to opposite connector.

7) Slide 8mm round crystal and a corrugated bead onto a head pin. Form a wrapped loop, attaching loop to end link of extender chain before wrapping. Trim excess wire. ●

Sources: Crystals from CRYSTALLIZED™ - Swarovski Elements; pearls and sunstone nuggets from Wraps Stones & Things; large necklace cone and corrugated beads from Great Craft Works; copper wire, German-style wire, head pins, rolo chain, jump rings, Wire Guardians, Victorian-style connectors, hook, crimp tubes, crimp covers and Bead Bumpers from Beadalon.

intermediate

PERSEPHONE

Design by Margot Potter

This earthy sumptuous palette of aged copper and brass, mossy greens and warm browns is the perfect choice for the cooler days of autumn. Focal shibuichi finish pendants and a single striking Kazuri ceramic bead combine with a variety of elements for a stunning effect. Mixed metals create surprisingly pleasing results.

INSTRUCTIONS

1) Using round-nose pliers and referring to Fig. 1, form loops at ends of 18-gauge wire to create an S hook. Open large end of hook and slide onto skeleton key and toggle round. ***Note:*** *Key will lie on front of pendant.*

Fig. 1

2) String a crimp bead onto beading wire ½ inch from end. Insert short wire tail through a brass ring and back through crimp bead, leaving a ½-inch loop to prevent wire wear. ***Note:*** *A Wire Guardian could also be used.* Use crimp pliers to flatten and fold crimp bead.

4) String a rondelle, rust/clear oval, rondelle and a smoky quartz coin. Repeat once. String a rondelle, rust/clear oval and rondelle. String S hook.

5) String rondelle, moss green oval, rondelle, grape bunch, moss green oval, grape bunch and rondelle.

6) String ceramic bead. Repeat step 5 in reverse.

7) String a crimp bead. Insert wire through second brass ring and back through crimp bead leaving a ½-inch loop. Flatten and fold crimp bead. Trim excess wire.

8) Use both pairs of chain-nose pliers to open end links of chain and attach to brass rings. Close links. ●

Sources: Shibuichi components from Green Girl Studios; ceramic bead from Kazuri West; Czech glass beads from York Novelty Imports Inc.; mini pendants from Blue Moon Beads; brass rings and chain from Ornamentea; crimp beads and wire from Beadalon.

MATERIALS

Czech glass beads: 4 (8mm) moss green ovals, 3 (6mm) two-tone rust/clear ovals, 12 (6mm) two-tone copper/rust rondelles
2 (6mm) smoky quartz flat coin beads
Rust/green ceramic bead
4 copper grape bunch mini pendants
2 wavy brass rings
Shibuichi components: skeleton key, Bird Over Clouds toggle round
2 (1.3mm) gold-plated crimp beads
1½ inches 18-gauge copper wire
9 inches .018-inch-diameter satin copper nylon-coated flexible beading wire
16½ inches large copper rolo chain
Round-nose pliers
2 pairs of chain-nose pliers
Crimp pliers
Wire cutters

FINISHED SIZE
24 inches

beginner

HOOT EARRINGS

Design by Andrew Thornton

Lustrous gunmetal-finish ear wires compliment the up-cycled bottle cap beads. Not only do these earrings "reduce, reuse and recycle," but they have a great sense of humor turning one man's trash into treasure with style.

INSTRUCTIONS

1) Slide a red coral rondelle and a bottle cap bead onto a head pin. Form a wrapped loop; trim excess wire. Open loop on ear wire and slide on beaded dangle; close loop.

2) Repeat step 1 for second earring. ⬤

Sources: Bottle cap beads from Glass Garden Beads; rondelles and head pins from Talisman Associates Inc.; ear wires from Saki Silver.

MATERIALS

2 (6mm) red coral rondelles
2 (15 x 22mm) owl bottle
   cap beads
2 (2½-inch) silver head pins
2 (20 x 38mm) gunmetal-finish
   almond-shaped ear wires

Round-nose pliers
Chain-nose pliers
Wire cutters

FINISHED SIZE
2⅝ inches long

beginner

OCTOBER'S JOURNEY

Design by Erin Strother

This rich autumn necklace features a focal pendant of carved golden horn leaves, complemented by the vivid colors of carnelian, smoky quartz, citrine, and red and green garnet.

INSTRUCTIONS

Project note: *If holes in leaf beads are too large for head pins, string a bronze seed bead onto head pin before stringing leaf bead.*

Pendant

1) On a 2-inch head pin, slide a leaf bead, garnet cylinder and an amber seed bead. Form a loop above beads. Trim excess wire. Open a 4mm jump ring and slide onto loop; attach jump ring to 10mm jump ring. Close ring.

2) On a 1-inch head pin, slide a bronze seed bead, ½ inch of green garnet chips and a bronze seed bead. Form a loop above beads. Trim excess wire. Attach to 10mm jump ring with a 4mm jump ring.

3) Cut a 1-inch length of chain. Open end link and attach to 10mm jump ring; close link. On a 1-inch head pin, slide a bronze seed bead, pearl, garnet rectangle and a bronze seed bead. Form a loop; trim excess wire. Open loop and attach to first link of 1-inch chain. Close loop.

4) On a 1-inch head pin, slide an amber seed bead, smoky quartz rondelle, pearl and a bronze seed bead. Form a loop. Trim excess wire. Open loop and attach to fifth link of chain; close loop.

5) Make another beaded dangle as in step 1. Open loop and attach to bottom link of chain. Close loop.

6) Cut a ½-inch length of chain. Open end link and attach to 10mm jump ring; close

Continued on page 91

MATERIALS

Golden horn beads: 3 (11 x 33mm) leaves, 4 (10mm) coins
Garnet beads: 11 (3mm) cylinders, 7 (5 x 3mm) rectangles
9 (7 x 4mm) smoky quartz faceted rondelles
2 (30 x 15mm) carnelian or red agate wavy oval beads
2 (20 x 15mm) citrine nugget beads
6½ inches green grossular garnet chips
3 (5mm) khaki CRYSTALLIZED™ - Swarovski Elements bicone crystals
5 gold freshwater pearls
11/0 seed beads: 13 metallic bronze, 9 amber

10mm copper heavyweight jump ring
4 (4mm) copper jump rings
Copper head pins: 3 (2-inch), 4 (1-inch)
2 copper crimp tubes
Copper S clasp
1½ inches copper cable chain
20 inches .018-inch-diameter nylon-coated flexible beading wire
Round-nose pliers
Chain-nose pliers
Flush cutters

FINISHED SIZE

18 inches (including clasp), plus a 3-inch pendant

SEPTEMBER RENDEZVOUS

Design by Fernando Dasilva, courtesy of Fernando Dasilva Jewelry

An over the top party filled with excitement, pleasure and spinning grooves inspired this design. Earthy and sparkling golden components create an incredible texturized effect softened by polyester chain.

Project note: *Use 6mm jump rings unless otherwise directed.*

INSTRUCTIONS

1) Slide a topaz crystal onto a head pin. Form a wrapped loop, sliding a twisted solid ring and a jump ring onto loop before wrapping. Trim excess wire. *Note: Use right portion of round-nose pliers when forming loop so loop is large enough to fit twisted ring.*

2) Repeat step 1 five more times for a total of six topaz dangles.

3) In the same manner as in step 1, make nine tiger's-eye dangles, seven crystal dorado dangles and five light Colorado topaz dangles. Set all dangles aside.

4) Attach a bail to each diamond drop. Set aside.

5) Open jump ring attached to one tiger's-eye dangle and slide it onto 27mm textured solid ring. Slide jump ring onto center link of chain. Close jump ring.

6) Open another jump ring and slide it onto 24mm textured solid ring and a diamond drop. Slide jump ring onto twisted solid ring from step 5. Close ring.

7) Open jump ring on a dangle and attach it to chain skipping one link from center dangle. Close ring. Continue in the same

Continued on page 91

MATERIALS
CRYSTALLIZED™ - Swarovski
  Elements bicone crystals:
  5 (8mm) light Colorado topaz,
  7 (8mm) crystal dorado,
  6 (10mm) topaz
2 (14 x 11 x 6mm) crystal copper
  CRYSTALLIZED™ - Swarovski
  Elements diamond drops
9 (12mm) tiger's-eye round beads
Gold charm with jump ring
2 gold-plated bails
Gold-plated jump rings:
  28 (6mm), 1 (4mm)
27 (16mm) gold-plated round
  twisted solid rings

Gold-plated textured solid rings:
  1 (27mm), 1 (24mm)
27 gold-plated medium ball-
  ended head pins
Gold-plated medium hook clasp
18½ inches brown
  polyester chain
Round-nose pliers
Chain-nose pliers
Flush cutters

FINISHED SIZE
19 inches (including clasp)

beginner

FRUiTS OF THE FOREST

Design by Melissa Lee

I found a strand of mixed seed pods at my local bead shop and couldn't resist the warm colors, shapes and textures of the beads. If you do not have precisely the same beads in your stash, try substituting with turquoise, olive jade, petrified opal, picture jasper, kukui nuts, lava or bronzite beads.

INSTRUCTIONS

1) String a crimp tube onto beading wire ½ inch from end. Insert short wire tail through loop on one half of clasp and back through crimp tube. Use crimp pliers to flatten crimp tube.

2) String the following, stringing a ceramic rondelle before each: seed pod, dark amber chunk, yellow turquoise bead, two light amber chunks, petrified wood slice, seed pod, seed pod, seed pod, three wooden beads, jade cube and wooden barrel bead. ***Note:*** *Do not separate groupings of the same beads with ceramic rondelles, such as the pair of light amber chunks and three wooden beads.*

3) String three ceramic rondelles, pendant and three ceramic rondelles.

4) String the following, stringing a ceramic rondelle after each: seed pod, seed pod, ocean amber chunk, yellow turquoise bead, garnet slice, amber barrel bead, seed pod, seed pod, three wooden beads, petrified wood slice and a seed pod. ***Note:*** *Do not separate grouping of three wooden beads with ceramic rondelles.*

5) String a crimp tube. Insert wire through remaining half of clasp and back through crimp tube and several other beads. Flatten and fold crimp tube. Trim excess wire. ●

Sources: Autumn Tree pendant from Melissa J. Lee; seed pods, yellow turqoise beads, dark and light amber chunks, amber barrel bead, ceramic rondelles and wooden barrel bead from Ayla's Originals; petrified wooden slices, wooden beads, garnet slice and turquoise clasp from AD Adornments; ocean amber beads and findings from Chelsea's Beads.

MATERIALS
Fine silver Autumn Tree pendant
9 (13–21 x 13–28mm) seed
   pod beads
10 x 12mm dark amber chunk
2 (23 x 32mm) light amber chunks
12 x 29mm ocean amber chunk
16 x 25mm amber barrel bead
2 (21mm) yellow turquoise
   round beads
2 (18 x 19mm) rough-cut
   petrified wood slice
6 (10 x 19mm) wooden beads
15 x 21mm nephrite jade
   cube bead
9 x 16mm) wooden barrel bead
22 x 24mm rough-cut garnet slice
28 (7mm) Raku ceramic rondelles
2 (2mm) sterling silver
   crimp tubes
Turquoise box clasp
25 inches .019-inch-diameter
   nylon-coated flexible
   beading wire
Crimp pliers
Wire cutters

FINISHED SIZE
22 inches (including clasp)

intermediate

AUTUMN TAKES FLiGHT

Design by Liz Revit

Get creative using resin charms to create these fabulous, lightweight earrings, adding whimsy to your autumn wardrobe. Swarovski crystals add just a touch of sparkle to these fun-to-wear earrings.

INSTRUCTIONS

1) Using both pairs of chain-nose pliers, open a jump ring and slide it onto a resin charm. Close ring.

2) Form a wrapped loop at one end of a 3-inch piece of wire, attaching loop to onto jump ring attached to charm before wrapping. String a pewter spacer, pearl and a pewter spacer. Form a wrapped loop. Trim excess wire.

3) Slide a bicone crystal onto a head pin. Form a wrapped loop. Trim excess wire. Repeat two more times for a total of three beaded dangles.

4) Open loop on ear wire. Slide on all three beaded dangles and wrapped loop above pearl. Close loop.

5) Repeat steps 1–4 for second earring. ●

Sources: Resin charms from Plaid Enterprises Inc.; pearls from Blue Moon Beads; pewter spacers from Talisman Associates Inc.; crystals, head pins and wire from Fusion Beads; ear wires and jump rings from Fire Mountain Gems and Beads.

MATERIALS
- 2 (¾ x ¾-inch) gold resin square charms
- 4 pewter spacers
- 2 (8mm) green pearls
- 4mm CRYSTALLIZED™ - Swarovski Elements bicone crystals: 2 light Colorado topaz, 2 topaz, 2 erinite
- 6 (1½-inch) 24-gauge sterling silver head pins
- 2 (7mm) silver-plated jump rings
- 2 sterling silver ear wires
- 2 (3-inch) lengths 20-gauge dead-soft sterling silver wire
- Round-nose pliers
- 2 pairs of chain-nose pliers
- Wire cutters

FINISHED SIZE
2¼ inches long

COPPER & SiLVER CHAiN

Continued from page 68

9) Repeat step 7 to attach silver chains to second, fourth and fifth circle links on 21-link chain.

10) Use an extra connector link to attach pendant to center (third) circle link on 21-link chain. Carefully open connector links on one side of center circle and slide on a silver chain; close links. Repeat to attach remaining silver chain to connector links on other side of center circle. Attach opposite ends of silver chains to single connector link attached to pendant. ●

Sources: Silver-plated bead from Jay's of Tucson; silver chain from Beadalon; copper chain from Crafts Etc!

AUTUMN SKiES

Continued from page 72

through remaining half of clasp and back through crimp tube. Use crimp pliers to flatten and fold crimp tube.

7) String a crystal copper rondelle, 20 pearls and crystal copper rondelle.

8) String a crimp tube. Insert wire through end links of two 1½-inch lengths of bar chain and one 1½-inch length of cable chain. Thread wire back through crimp tube. Flatten and fold crimp tube. Trim excess wire.

9) Cut a 1½-inch length of brown wire. Form a wrapped loop, attaching loop to ends of chains from step 8 before wrapping. String a golden coral round bead. Form another wrapped loop, attaching loop to two 1½-inch lengths of bar chain and one 1½-inch length of cable chain before wrapping. Trim excess wire.

10) Repeat step 9 two more times, attaching links to previous chains. **Note:** *For last set, substitute 1-inch chains in place of 1½-inch chains.*

11) Insert remaining 2-inch brown wire through pendant holes centering pendant on wire. Thread one wire end through opposite hole and pull wire to secure pendant. Bring wire ends up above pendant; wrap shorter wire around base of longer wire. Form longer wire into a wrapped loop, catching ends of 1-inch chains and wire-wrapped link chains on loop before wrapping. Trim excess wire.

12) Slide goldstone bead onto head pin; form a wrapped loop, attaching loop to wrapped loop above pendant before wrapping. Trim excess wire. ●

Sources: Pendant from Pam & Heather Wynn; pearls, goldstone bead and golden coral beads from Talisman Associates Inc.; head pin from E2S Supplies; CRYSTALLIZED™ - Swarovski Elements crystals, crimp tubes and beading wire from Fusion Beads; toggle clasp from Green Girl Studios; chain from Ornamentea.

OCTOBER'S jOURNEY

Continued from page 82

link. On a 1-inch head pin, slide a bronze seed bead, bicone crystal and a bronze seed bead. Form a loop. Trim excess wire. Open loop and attach to second link of ½-inch chain. Close loop.

7) On a 2-inch head pin, slide a leaf bead, garnet cylinder, bronze seed bead and a pearl. Form a loop. Trim excess wire. Open loop and attach to last link of chain; close loop. Set pendant aside.

Necklace

1) Open a 4mm jump ring and attach to round half of clasp; close ring.

2) String a crimp tube onto beading wire ½ inch from one end. Place short wire tail through 4mm jump ring attached to clasp and back through crimp tube. Use crimp pliers to flatten and fold crimp tube.

3) String the following: three amber seed beads, bronze seed bead, garnet rectangle, 2¼ inches green garnet chips, garnet rectangle, golden horn coin, smoky quartz rondelle, ¾ inch green garnet chips, garnet rectangle, citrine nugget, pearl, carnelian oval, golden horn coin, three smoky quartz rondelles, bicone crystal and four garnet cylinders.

4) String pendant.

5) Repeat step 3 in reverse.

6) Open a 4mm jump ring and attach to S half of clasp; close ring.

7) String a crimp tube onto beading wire. Place wire end through previous 4mm jump ring and back through crimp tube and several other beads. Flatten and fold crimp tube. Trim excess wire. ●

Sources: Golden horn beads from Beads and Pieces; citrine and carnelian beads from South Sun Products Inc.; smoky quartz beads and bicone crystals from Fusion Beads; garnet chips from Artbeads.com; garnet beads, pearls, seed beads, copper chain and findings from Beadaholique.

SEPTEMBER RENDEZVOUS

Continued from page 84

manner to attach 13 dangles on each side of center dangle skipping one link between each.

8) Open 4mm jump ring and slide it onto hook clasp; attach jump ring to one end of chain. Close ring.

9) Open jump ring attached to charm and slide on remaining diamond drop. Attach jump ring to opposite end of chain; close ring. ●

Sources: Crystal components from CRYSTALLIZED™ - Swarovski Elements; tiger's-eye beads from Wraps Stones & Things; solid textured and twisted rings, head pins, jump rings and polyester chain from Beadalon.

WiNTER

*Cool tones hint of winter temperatures,
and jewel tones tell tales of big, passionate
holidays. Celebrate Christmas, Hanukkah,
New Year's, Martin Luther King Day,
Valentine's Day, Groundhog Day and
a score of presidential birthdays.*

HAPPY HOLiDAY EARRiNGS

Design by Melissa Lee

I wanted to do something a little unusual with bead cones and decided that the classic shape could be used sculpturally, instead. Try out different styles of bead cones to create different decorated "trees."

INSTRUCTIONS

1) Slide the following onto a head pin: brown cube, five seed beads, garnet crystal, bead cone (wide end facing down), garnet crystal and glass star.

2) Form a wrapped loop above star; trim excess wire. Open loop on ear wire and slide on beaded dangle. Close loop.

3) Repeat steps 1 and 2 for second earring. ●

Source: Venetian glass beads, seed beads, crystals, bead cones and findings from Bruce Frank Beads.

MATERIALS

2 (15 x 15mm) sterling silver bead cones
Venetian glass gold-foil beads: 2 (13mm) blue stars, 2 (6mm) brown cubes
4 (4mm) garnet CRYSTALLIZED™ - Swarovski Elements bicone crystals
10 (11/0) red seed beads
2 (3-inch) 24-gauge sterling silver head pins
2 sterling silver ear wires
Round-nose pliers
Chain-nose pliers
Flush cutters

FINISHED SIZE

2¼ inches long

beginner

PEPPERMiNT TWiST

Design by Caito Amorose

A hard candy treat is a bracelet that looks good enough to eat. Just a few quick wrapped loops transform a holiday favorite into a refreshingly sweet accessory with zero calories!

INSTRUCTIONS

1) Slide a seed bead, red/white striped bead and a light siam crystal onto a head pin. Form a wrapped loop, attaching loop to first link of chain before wrapping. Trim excess wire.

2) Repeat step 1 attaching dangle to chain approximately 1¼ inches from first dangle.

3) Repeat step 1 six more times, attaching dangles to chain approximately ¾ inch apart. ***Note:*** *Attach last dangle to last link of chain.*

4) Form a wrapped loop at one end of 24-gauge wire attaching loop to last link of chain before wrapping. String a light siam crystal, peppermint candy bead and a light siam crystal. Form a wrapped loop. Trim excess wire.

5) Slide clasp onto split ring. Attach split ring to previous wrapped loop. ●

Sources: Lampwork bead and glass beads from Goody Beads; crystals, seed beads, findings, chain and wire from Fire Mountain Gems and Beads.

MATERIALS
10 (4mm) light siam
   CRYSTALLIZED™ - Swarovski
   Elements bicone crystals
20 x 15 x 9mm peppermint
   candy lampwork bead
8 (4 x 8mm) red/white striped
   round glass beads
8 (11/0) silver seed beads
8 (1-inch) sterling silver head pins
Sterling silver split ring
Sterling silver lobster-claw clasp
3 inches 24-gauge sterling
   silver wire
6⅛ inches sterling silver 6mm
   figure-eight chain
Round-nose pliers
Chain-nose pliers
Wire cutters

FINISHED SIZE
7¾ inches
   (including clasp)

SNOWFLAKE ELEGANCE

Designs by Melanie Brooks Lukacs, courtesy of Earthenwood Studio

Warm black velvet and cool porcelain combine to make a necklace that is bound to help take the chill off in the snowy days of winter.

INSTRUCTIONS

Snowflake Dangles

1) Use both pairs of chain-nose pliers to open a 7mm jump ring. Insert jump ring through one side at bottom of a sterling silver snowflake charm. Slide porcelain charm onto jump ring. Close ring. Repeat to attach another 7mm jump ring to porcelain charm, sliding jump ring through other side of sterling silver snowflake.

2) Open a 5mm jump ring and slide on a pyramid charm. Insert jump ring through 7mm jump rings attached to porcelain charm. Close ring.

3) Repeat steps 1 and 2 two more times to make a total of three snowflake dangles. Set aside.

Necklace

1) String a crimp tube onto wire ½ inch from one end. Insert short wire tail through loop on toggle bar and back

through crimp tube. Use crimp pliers to flatten and fold crimp tube. Trim short wire up next to crimp tube. Attach a crimp cover over crimp tube using chain-nose pliers to close.

2) String a pewter spacer, 6-inch velour tubing and a pewter spacing.

Continued on page 116

MATERIALS

- 3 (16mm) black-and-white porcelain snowflake charms
- 3 (12 x 17mm) sterling silver snowflake charms
- 4 (10 x 12mm) jet black porcelain pebble beads
- 2 (14mm) black-and-white lava tab beads
- 16 (4mm) alabaster white CRYSTALLIZED™ - Swarovski Elements bicone crystals
- 16 (4mm) silver-plated beaded pewter spacer beads
- 11 (5mm) silver-plated pewter pyramid charms
- 10 x 7mm silver-plated pewter beaded bail
- Sterling silver jump rings: 4 (5mm), 6 (7mm)
- 2 (2 x 2mm) sterling silver crimp tubes
- 2 (3mm) sterling silver crimp covers
- 2 sterling silver ear wires
- 11 x 14mm silver-plated pewter beaded toggle clasp
- 2 (6-inch) lengths 3mm black velour tubing
- 24 inches .018-inch-diameter nylon-coated flexible beading wire
- 2 pairs of chain-nose pliers
- Crimp pliers
- Wire cutters

FINISHED SIZES

Necklace
18½ inches (including clasp)

Earrings
2 inches long

intermediate

CECiLY

Designs by Molly Schaller

Foil-backed crystals hang between cut glass beads for a decidedly French look punctuated with wire-wrapped marquise-shaped dangles.

INSTRUCTIONS

Necklace

1) Pass a 2-inch eye pin through an oval marquise bead and position bead approximately ½ inch from loop on eye pin. Bend both sides of pin centered above bead. Wrap long wire tail around base of eye-pin loop securing bead to pin. Trim excess wire.

2) Repeat step 1 with 23 oval marquise beads for a total of 24 oval marquise drops.

3) Slide a teardrop bead onto a 1-inch eye pin. Form a loop. Trim excess wire. Repeat with 23 teardrop beads for a total of 24 teardrop links.

4) Open a 6mm jump ring and slide it through a crystal; close ring. Repeat with nine crystals for a total of 10 crystal drops.

5) Slide a silver round bead, rondelle and a silver round bead onto a 1-inch eye pin. Form a loop. Trim excess wire to create a rondelle link.

6) Open a 6mm jump ring and slide it onto large pendant and one loop of rondelle link. Close ring.

7) To assemble necklace, open a 4mm jump ring and slide the following onto it: one teardrop link, two oval marquise drops and one teardrop link. Close ring.

8) Open another 4mm jump ring and slide it onto opposite loop of previous teardrop link. Slide a crystal drop and another teardrop link onto jump ring. Close ring.

9) Open another 4mm jump ring and slide it onto opposite loop of previous teardrop link. Slide two oval marquis drops and one teardrop link onto jump ring. Close ring.

Continued on page 117

MATERIALS

15 (12mm) foil-backed faceted smoke crystals
34 (8 x 12mm) smooth jet black glass teardrop beads
36 (8 x 15mm) faceted jet black glass oval marquise beads
3 x 6mm faceted jet black glass rondelle
2 (3mm) silver round beads
Faceted jet black glass pendants: 1 (37 x 22mm), 1 (20 x 30mm)
Silver eye pins: 36 (2-inch), 35 (1-inch)
Silver jump rings: 19 (6mm), 34 (4mm)
2 (12 x 6mm) silver swivel lobster-claw clasps
Round-nose pliers
Chain-nose pliers
Flush cutters

FINISHED SIZES

Necklace
16 inches (including clasp) with a 2-inch pendant

Bracelet
7 inches (including clasp)

intermediate

EVENiNG STARLiGHT

Design by Andrew Thornton

A winter wonderland fringed with icicles twinkles gently in the starlight. Mixing cool tones and striking gold, these sophisticated and sexy earrings sparkle and shine.

INSTRUCTIONS

1) Cut a 1½-inch piece of wire. Form a wrapped loop at one end, attaching loop to ear-wire loop before wrapping. String a 5 x 7mm oval pearl. Form a wrapped loop. Trim excess wire.

2) Cut a 1-inch piece of wire. Form a wrapped loop at one end, attaching loop to previous loop before wrapping. String a bicone crystal. Form a wrapped loop. Trim excess wire.

3) Cut a 2-inch piece of wire. Form a wrapped loop at one end, attaching loop to previous loop before wrapping. String teardrop bead. Wrap wire tail around top of bead and loop securing bead to wire. Trim excess wire.

4) Slide a 5 x 3mm pearl onto a head pin. Form a wrapped loop, attaching loop to loop above teardrop bead before wrapping. Trim excess wire. Repeat to attach a 4 x 3mm pearl to loop.

5) Repeat steps 1–4 for second earring. ●

Sources: Pearls and Czech glass beads from Talisman Associates Inc.; bicone crystals and wire from Fusion Beads; ear wires from Saki Silver.

MATERIALS
2 (5 x 7mm) white oval pearls
2 (4mm) clear CRYSTALLIZED™ - Swarovski Elements bicone crystals
2 (4 x 3mm) white center-drilled rice pearls
2 (5 x 3mm) white vertically-drilled rice pearls
2 (13 x 9mm) clear Czech glass top-drilled teardrop beads

4 (1-inch) sterling silver head pins
2 (40 x 20mm) sterling silver almond-shaped ear wires
9 inches 24-gauge dead-soft gold-filled wire
Round-nose pliers
Chain-nose pliers
Flush cutters

FINISHED SIZE
3¼ inches long

beginner

jE T'ADORE

Design by Brenda Morris Jarrett

Hearts are the universal symbol of love. Add an adorable "I love you" charm and the recipient will truly feel special.

INSTRUCTIONS

1) Slide the following onto head pin: 2mm sterling silver bead, 3mm sterling silver bead, spacer bead and a 6mm bicone crystal.

2) Insert head pin through bottom of bead frame. Slide a 6mm bicone crystal, spacer bead and a 4mm bicone crystal onto head pin. These beads will sit inside bead frame.

3) Continue to thread head pin through top of bead frame.

4) String a 4mm bicone crystal, charm, spacer bead, 3mm sterling silver bead and a 2mm sterling silver bead.

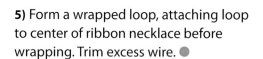

5) Form a wrapped loop, attaching loop to center of ribbon necklace before wrapping. Trim excess wire. ●

Sources: Crystals, sterling silver beads, spacers, bead frame and head pin from Fire Mountain Gems and Beads; charm from Hobby Lobby Stores Inc.; silk ribbon necklace from Thunderbird Supply Co.

MATERIALS
CRYSTALLIZED™ - Swarovski
  Elements bicone crystals:
    2 (6mm) siam satin,
    2 (4mm) siam
Sterling silver round beads:
    2 (3mm), 2 (2mm)
3 (5 x 1.3mm) sterling silver
    spacer beads
Sterling silver "I love you" charm
15mm sterling silver open heart
    bead frame

3-inch sterling silver head pin
16-inch black silk ribbon necklace
    with sterling silver clasp
Round-nose pliers
Needle-nose pliers
Flush cutters

FINISHED SIZE
16 inches (including clasp)

OH MY BEADiNG HEART

Design by Suzann Wilson

The love of beading takes flight with a necklace that is perfect for Valentine's Day or any day of the year.

INSTRUCTIONS

1) Use both pairs of chain-nose pliers to open jump ring and slide it onto pendant; close ring. Set aside.

2) String a crimp tube onto wire ½ inch from one end. Thread short wire tail through loop on one half of clasp and back through crimp tube. Use crimp pliers to flatten and fold crimp tube. Trim short wire tail close to crimp tube.

3) String a filigree bead and a jet bead.

4) String a daisy spacer, cylinder bumpy bead, daisy spacer, jet bead, filigree bead and jet bead.

5) String a daisy spacer, round bumpy bead, daisy spacer, jet bead, filigree bead and jet bead.

6) Repeat steps 4 and 5. Repeat step 4.

7) String a daisy spacer, pendant and a daisy spacer.

8) Repeat steps 3–6 in reverse to complete other half of necklace.

9) String a crimp tube. Thread wire through loop on remaining half of clasp and back through crimp tube. Flatten and fold crimp tube. Trim excess wire. ●

Sources: Pendant from Earthenwood Studio; bumpy beads from Ideal Supply House Inc.; Czech glass beads from ABC Direct; clasp from Super Time International; crimp tubes and beading wire from Beadalon.

MATERIALS
22 (8mm) jet black Czech glass fire-polished beads
Red/black/white bumpy glass beads: 6 (9 x 10mm) cylinder, 4 (9mm) round
12 silver filigree cylinder or tube beads
22 silver daisy spacers
Heartflight ceramic pendant
4mm silver jump ring
2 (2mm) silver crimp tubes
Silver toggle clasp
22 inches .015-inch-diameter 19-strand nylon-coated flexible beading wire
2 pairs of chain-nose pliers
Crimp pliers
Wire cutters

FINISHED SIZE
19 inches (including clasp)

PURE PASSiON

Design by Barb Switzer

Perfect for a romantic evening, wedding or any dress event, this necklace highlights classic pearls with a punch of ruby boldness. Gold findings add formality and richness.

INSTRUCTIONS

1) Slide a red crystal, daisy spacer and a pearl onto a head pin. Form a wrapped loop. Trim excess wire. Repeat four more times for a total of five beaded dangles. Set aside.

2) String a crimp tube and a daisy spacer onto beading wire ½ inch from end. Insert short wire tail through one half of clasp. Thread wire end back through daisy spacer and crimp tube. Use crimp pliers to flatten and fold crimp tube.

3) String a daisy spacer, red crystal and a daisy spacer.

4) Beginning and ending with a seed bead, string six seed beads and five pearls alternating between the two.

5) Repeat step 3.

6) In the same manner as in step 4, string eight seed beads and seven pearls.

7) String a daisy spacer, three red crystals and a daisy spacer.

8) Repeat steps 4 and 3.

9) In the same manner as in step 4, string four seed beads and three pearls.

10) String a daisy spacer, red crystal, beaded dangle, red crystal, daisy spacer and a pearl. Repeat once. String a daisy spacer, red crystal and a daisy spacer.

11) String a beaded dangle.

12) Repeat steps 3–10 in reverse to string remaining half of necklace.

13) String a crimp tube and a daisy spacer. Insert wire through other half of clasp and back through daisy spacer, crimp tube and several other beads. Flatten and fold crimp tube. Trim excess wire. ●

Source: Beads, crystals, pearls, findings, clasp and beading wire from Fusion Beads.

MATERIALS
35 gold-plated daisy spacers
27 (3mm) red bicone crystals
49 (5–6mm) white freshwater pearls
48 (11/0) gold seed beads
5 gold-filled head pins
2 (1.3mm) gold-filled crimp tubes
Gold-filled toggle clasp
20 inches .014-inch-diameter nylon-coated flexible beading wire
Round-nose pliers
Chain-nose pliers
Wire cutters

FINISHED SIZE
17½ inches (including clasp)

jANUARY THAW

Design by Erin Strother

One aqua rectangle stands alone with five icy-white faceted chalcedony nuggets in this simple, elegant piece that is somehow chunky and delicate all at once. The circle chain makes the necklace adjustable for length.

INSTRUCTIONS

1) Cut a 1¾-inch length of wire. Form a wrapped loop at one end. String a 7mm pearl and form another wrapped loop. Trim excess wire. Repeat three times for a total of four pearl links.

2) Cut a 2¼-inch length of wire. Form a wrapped loop at one end. String a white chalcedony nugget and form another wrapped loop. Trim excess wire. Repeat five more times, four times with white chalcedony nuggets and once with aqua chalcedony rectangle.

3) Open a jump ring and slide it onto clasp and one end of a pearl link. Close ring.

4) Continue to use jump rings to connect the following to form necklace: six links of chain, white nugget link, two links of chain, aqua rectangle link, two white nugget links, one link of chain, white nugget link, pearl link, white nugget link, three links of chain, two pearl links and six links of chain.

5) Slide aquamarine rectangle and 3mm pearl onto a head pin. Form a loop. Trim excess wire. Open loop and attach to last chain link. Close loop.

6) Slide a 7mm pearl onto a head pin. Form a loop. Trim excess wire. Open loop and attach to single link of chain between white nugget links. Close loop. ●

Sources: Chalcedony beads from Beadaholique; pearls, aquamarine bead, chain, wire and findings from Fire Mountain Gems and Beads.

MATERIALS
Faceted chalcedony beads:
   5 (18 x 15mm) white nuggets,
   1 (17 x 13mm) aqua rectangle
White pearls: 5 (7mm), 1 (3mm)
5 x 4mm aquamarine
   rectangle bead
2 (1-inch) sterling silver head pins
15 (4mm) sterling silver
   jump rings
Sterling silver hook clasp

20½ inches 24-gauge
   sterling silver wire
18 links sterling silver
   10mm round circle chain
Round-nose pliers
Chain-nose pliers
Flush cutters

FINISHED SIZE
17 inches (including clasp)

GLACiER BAY

Design by Erin Strother

A frosty cascade of silvery-blue translucent kyanite, clear crystal quartz and sterling silver completes these delicate earrings. These are perfect for a holiday party, or to dress up jeans and a white shirt.

INSTRUCTIONS

1) Open a jump ring and slide on two more jump rings. Close ring. Open one of the end rings and attach to loop on ear wire; close ring.

2) Cut an 8-inch length of wire. String a small kyanite stick 1 inch from wire end. Bring both wire ends centered above bead. Wrap shorter wire around base of long wire three times. Trim short wire tail. Form a wrapped loop with long wire wrapping it back down over wire coils. Keep wrapping wire down around bead as desired. Trim excess wire. Use chain-nose pliers to flatten wire end against bead.

3) Repeat step 2 with a large kyanite stick.

4) Open top jump ring and slide on large kyanite stick; close ring. Repeat to attach small kyanite stick to bottom jump ring.

5) Slide a seed bead and a rondelle onto a head pin. Form a wrapped loop above beads, attaching loop to top jump ring before wrapping. Trim excess wire.

6) Repeat step 5 two more times attaching beaded dangles to second and third jump rings.

7) Repeat steps 1–6 for second earring. ●

Source: Pendants, beads, wire and findings from Beadaholique.

MATERIALS
Blue kyanite stick pendants:
  2 (15–16mm), 2 (17–18mm)
6 (5mm) crystal quartz rondelles
6 (11/0) light blue silver-lined
  seed beads
6 (1-inch) sterling silver head pins
6 (7mm) sterling silver jump rings
2 sterling silver ear wires

32 inches 24-gauge sterling
  silver wire
Round-nose pliers
Chain-nose pliers
Flush cutters

FINISHED SIZE
2 inches long

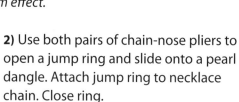

WiNTER WHiTES

Design by Margot Potter

The base for this bold and beautiful re-crafted vintage necklace was an affordable find at a local estate auction. Extra-large vintage faux pearls and plastic geometric beads in off-white are piled onto the existing faux pearls for maximum effect.

Project notes: *Look for vintage necklaces at estate sales, local thrift shops, flea markets and online. If you cannot find a vintage necklace with pearls, create pearl dangles on head pins and attach them to a necklace chain with jump rings.*

INSTRUCTIONS

1) Slide a bead cap, 20mm pearl and a bead cap onto a head pin. ***Note:*** *String bead caps so they "cup" the pearl.* Form a wrapped loop above bead cap. Trim excess wire. Repeat with each 20mm pearl.

2) Use both pairs of chain-nose pliers to open a jump ring and slide onto a pearl dangle. Attach jump ring to necklace chain. Close ring.

3) Continue using jump rings to attach pearl dangles and geometric pendants to chain as desired. ●

Sources: Large faux pearls and vintage plastic pendants from The Impatient Crafter; bead caps and findings from Beadalon.

MATERIALS

Vintage necklace with various
   sizes of attached white
   faux pearls
10 (20mm) white faux pearls
10 off-white vintage plastic
   geometric pendants
20 gold-plated leaf motif
   bead caps

10 gold-plated head pins
20 (8mm) gold-plated jump rings
Round-nose pliers
2 pairs of chain-nose pliers
Flush cutters

FINISHED SIZE
18½ inches (including clasp)

SNOWFLAKE ELEGANCE

Continued from page 98

3) String a bicone crystal, pyramid charm and a bicone crystal.

4) String a pewter spacer, pebble bead and a pewter spacer.

5) Repeat step 3.

6) String a pewter lava tab bead and a pewter spacer.

7) Repeat steps 3 and 4. Repeat step 3.

8) String beaded bail.

9) Repeat steps 2–7 in reverse to string other half of necklace.

10) String a crimp tube. Insert wire through loop on round half of clasp and back through crimp tube. Flatten and fold crimp tube. Trim wire. Attach a crimp cover over crimp tube.

11) Open a 5mm jump ring and slide onto one snowflake dangle. Attach jump ring to loop on beaded bail. Close ring.

Earrings

1) Open loops on ear wires and slide on remaining two snowflake dangles. Close loops. ●

Sources: Porcelain charms and beads from Earthenwood Studio; sterling silver charms from Rio Grande; ear wires from Nina Designs; velour tubing from Shipwreck Beads; lava tab beads, crystals, pewter components, jump rings, crimp tubes, crimp covers, clasp and beading wire from Fusion Beads.

CECiLY

Continued from page 100

10) Repeat steps 8 and 9 four more times. This completes one side of necklace.

11) Repeat steps 7–10 to complete second side of necklace.

12) Open a 4mm jump ring and slide it onto teardrop links at one end of both sides of necklace. This is center of necklace. Slide rondelle link onto center jump ring. Close ring.

13) Open a 4mm jump ring and pass it through clasp and final link on one side of necklace; close ring. Open a 6mm jump ring and slide it onto final link at opposite side of necklace; close ring.

Bracelet

1) Follow step 1 of Necklace to make a total of 12 oval marquise drops.

2) Follow step 3 of Necklace to make a total of 10 teardrop links.

3) Follow step 4 of Necklace to make a total of 5 crystal drops.

4) Open a 6mm jump ring and slide it onto small pendant; close ring.

5) To assemble bracelet, open a 4mm jump ring and place it onto clasp, two oval marquise drops and one teardrop link. Close jump ring.

6) Open another 4mm jump ring and slide it onto opposite end of previous teardrop link. Slide a crystal drop and a teardrop link onto jump ring. Close ring.

7) Open another 4mm jump ring and slide it onto opposite link of previous teardrop link. Slide two oval marquise drops and one teardrop link onto jump ring. Close ring.

8) Repeat steps 6 and 7 three more times. Repeat step 6.

9) Open a 6mm jump ring and slide it through last teardrop link. Slide two oval marquise drops and pendant onto jump ring. Close ring. ●

Sources: All beads from Halcraft USA; eye pins and jump rings from Beadalon.

ALL SEASONS

Turn a basic idea into jewelry for every season by starting with a beautiful simple design and filling in the blanks. Versatile interchangeable designs make a perfect style statement any time year.

beginner

SEASONS CHANGE PENDANT

Design by Andrew Thornton

The bright, saturated candy colors of the resin loops and seasonally inspired wire-wrapped embellished dangles make for versatile components that can be readily swapped out or added to another piece according to mood or season.

INSTRUCTIONS

1) Slide a 4mm round bead onto a head pin. Pass head pin through top hole of resin ring with bead on the inside of the ring. Form a wrapped loop on outside of ring forming a wrapped bail. Trim excess wire.

2) Form a wrapped loop at one end of 24-gauge wire, attaching loop to wrapped bail from step 1 before wrapping. String 6mm rondelle. Form another wrapped loop, attaching loop to clasp before wrapping. Trim excess wire.

3) Slide a 4mm round bead onto a head pin. Pass head pin through bottom hole of resin ring with bead on the inside of the ring. Form a wrapped loop on outside of ring, attaching loop to end link of chain before wrapping.

4) Slide one or two beads onto a head pin. Form a wrapped loop above beads, attaching loop to chain before wrapping. Trim excess wire. Repeat with remaining head pins to embellish chain.

5) Attach pendant to chain or ribbon necklace. ●

Sources: Resin ring from Natural Touch Beads; chain, clasp, head pins and wire from Fusion Beads.

MATERIALS
39mm resin round ring with
    top- and bottom-drilled holes
6mm rondelle
2 (4mm) round beads
20–26 assorted beads
    and crystals
15 (1½-inch) sterling silver
    head pins
7 x 13mm silver lobster-claw clasp
1½ inches 5 x 6mm silver cable
    chain (7 links)
1 inch 24-gauge half-hard
    sterling silver wire
Ribbon or chain necklace
    with clasp
Round-nose pliers
Chain-nose pliers
Flush cutters

FINISHED SIZE
4½ inches long

beginner

CHANGEABLE PENDANT

Design by Candie Cooper

A compelling group of elements and focal pendants create four groups perfect for every time of year.

INSTRUCTIONS

1) Open a jump ring and pass it through one hole of pendant. Slide a bead or charm onto jump ring. Close ring. ***Note:*** *A piece of leather cord can also be tied through hole creating a ring.*

2) Slide assorted beads onto a head pin or eye pin. Form a loop after beads. Trim excess wire. Repeat as desired.

3) Slide beaded dangles and charms onto a jump ring. Pass jump ring through bottom hole of pendant. Close ring. ***Note:*** *A second jump ring can be used to attach beaded dangles and charms if desired.*

4) To wear, slide pendant onto necklace chain. ●

Sources: Resin pendants, charms and jump rings from Plaid Enterprises Inc.; head pins and leather cord from Beadalon.

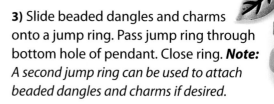

MATERIALS

Resin pendant
Assorted beads and crystals
Charms
Head pins and/or eye pins
2–3 (10mm) jump rings
Leather cord (optional)

Necklace chain
Round-nose pliers
Chain-nose pliers
Flush cutters

FINISHED SIZE

3–4 inches long

PHOTO iNDEX

PHOTO iNDEX

FALL

Halloween Bracelet, 66

Copper & Silver Chain, 68

Indian Summer, 70

Autumn Skies, 72

Saint Laurent Tassel, 74

Persephone, 78

Hoot Earrings, 80

October's Journey, 82

September Rendezvous, 84

Fruits of the Forest, 86

Autumn Takes Flight, 88

WiNTER

Happy Holiday Earrings, 94

Peppermint Twist, 96

Snowflake Elegance, 98

Cecily, 100

Evening Starlight, 102

Je T'Adore, 104

Oh My Beading Heart, 106

Pure Passion, 108

January Thaw, 110

Glacier Bay, 112

Winter Whites, 114

ALL SEASONS

Seasons Change Pendants, 120
Changeable Pendant, 122

BUYER'S GUIDE

Due to the ever-changing nature of the bead industry, it may be impossible to find the exact beads and components used in the designs shown in this publication. Similar beads may be found via the Internet or by visiting your local bead shops and shows.

ABC Direct
(877) 696-9490
www.abcdirectbeads.com

AD Adornments
www.adadornments.com

Artbeads.com
(866) 715-2323
www.artbeads.com

Ayla's Originals
(877) 328-AYLA (2952)
www.aylasoriginals.com

Bead Addicts
www.beadaddicts.etsy.com

Beadalon
(866) 4BEADALON (423-2325)
www.beadalon.com

Beads and Pieces
(800) 652-3237
www.beadsandpieces.com

Beadaholique
www.beadaholique.com

Blue Moon Beads
(800) 727-2727
www.creativityinc.com/
bluemoonbeads.

Brass Bouquet
(877) 346-7348
www.brassbouquet.com

Brightlings Beads
(919) 388-9822
www.brightlingsbeads.com

Bruce Frank Beads
(877) BEADS-75 (232-3775)
www.brucefrankbeads.com

Caravan Beads Inc.
www.caravanbeads.com

Chelsea's Beads
(847) 433-3451
www.chelseasbeads.com

Cousin Corp. of America
(800) 366-2687
www.cousin.com

CR Enterprises
www.crenterprises.firm.in

Crafts Etc!
(800) 888-0321
www.craftsetc.com

CRYSTALLIZED™ - Swarovski Elements
www.create-your-style.com

E2S Supplies
www.e2ssupplies.etsy.com

E. A. Revit Inc.
(570) 287-1376

Earthenwood Studio
(248) 548-4793
www.earthenwoodstudio.com

Every Heart Crafts
www.everyheartcrafts.etsy.com

Fernando Dasilva Jewelry
(214) 766-8354
www.dasilvajewelry.com

Fire Mountain Gems and Beads
(800) 355-2137
www.firemountaingems.com

Frabels Inc.
www.frabels.com

Fusion Beads
www.fusionbeads.com

Gemshow-Online Jewelry Supply
(877) 805-7440
www.gemshow-online.com

Glass Garden Beads
(507) 645-0301
www.glassgardenbeads.com

Goody Beads
(952) 938-2324
www.goodybeads.com

Great Craft Works
(610) 431-9790
www.greatcraftworks.com

Green Girl Studios
(828) 298-2263
www.greengirlstudios.com

Halcraft USA
(914) 840-0505
www.halcraft.com

Hobby Lobby Stores Inc.
www.hobbylobby.com

Ideal Supply House Inc.
(678) 560-6868
www.ebeadstore.com

The Impatient Crafter
www.etsy.com/shop.
php?user_id=5584835

Jangles
(706) 207-9032
www.jangles.net

Jay's of Tucson
(800) 736-6381
www.jays-of-tucson.com

Jo-Ann Stores Inc.
(888) 739-4120
www.joann.com

Joan Miller Porcelain Beads
www.joanmiller.com

John Bead Corp.
(888) 755-9055
www.johnbead.com

Kazuri West
www.kazuriwest.com

The LH Bead Gallery
(850) 257-5800
www.lhbeads.com

Lily Studios
www.lilystudios.net

Majestic Pearl Inc.
(212) 268-9881
www.majesticpearl.com

Melissa J. Lee
www.melissajlee.etsy.com

Michaels Stores Inc.
www.michaels.com

Michele Goldstein
www.michelegoldstein.com

Natural Touch Beads
(707) 781-0808
www.naturaltouchbeads.com

Nina Designs
(800) 336-6462
www.ninadesigns.com

Ornamentea
(919) 834-6260
www.ornamentea.com

Oriental Trading Co.
(800) 875-8480
www.orientaltrading.com

Pam & Heather Wynn
www.heatherwynn.com

Pegasus Imports
(800) 742-2323
www.pegasusimports.com

Plaid Enterprises Inc.
(800) 842-4197
www.plaidonline.com

The Ring Lord
(306) 374-1335
www.theringlord.com

Rings & Things
(800) 366-2156
www.rings-things.com

Rio Grande
www.riogrande.com

RupaB Designs
(510) 791-6135
www.rupab.com

Sajen Inc.
(800) 772-5369
www.sajenjewelry.com

Saki Silver
(513) 221-5480
www.sakisilver.com

Shipwreck Beads
(800) 950-4232
www.shipwreckbeads.com

Shogun Trading Co. Inc.
(800) 458-8004
www.shogunpearl.com

Somerset Silver Inc.
(800) 281-1170
www.somerset-silver.com

Soft Flex Co.
(866) 925-FLEX (925-3539)
www.softflexcompany.com

South Sun Products Inc.
(858) 309-5045
www.southsunproducts.com

Super Time International
(800) 878-2943
www.supertimebeads.com

Sweet Creek Inc.
(541) 997-0109
www.sweetcreek.com

Talisman Associates Inc.
(800) 229-7890
www.talismanbeads.com

Thunderbird Supply Co.
(800) 545-7968
www.thunderbirdsupply.com

Tucson Mountain Jewelry/LS Designs
www.tucsonmountain
jewels.com

VenetianBeadShop.com
(800) 439-3551
www.venetianbeadshop.com

Village Originals Inc.
(407) 855-4004
www.villageoriginals.com

Wraps Stones & Things
(415) 863-4953
www.beadsnclasps.com

York Novelty Imports Inc.
(800) 223-6676
www.yorkbeads.com

The Buyer's Guide listings are provided as a service to our readers and should not be considered an endorsement from this publication.

SPECiAL THANKS